SHARKS
FOREVER

The Mystery and History of the Planet's Perfect Predator

SHARKS FOREVER

The Mystery and History of the Planet's Perfect Predator

MARK LEIREN-YOUNG

ORCA BOOK PUBLISHERS

Published in Canada and the United States
in 2022 by Orca Book Publishers.
orcabook.com

Library and Archives Canada Cataloguing in Publication
Title: Sharks forever : the mystery and history of the
planet's perfect predator / Mark Leiren-Young.
Names: Leiren-Young, Mark, author.
Series: Orca wild ; 9.
Description: Series statement: Orca wild ; 9 |
Includes bibliographical references and index.
Identifiers: Canadiana (print) 20210365986 |
Canadiana (ebook) 20210365994 | ISBN 9781459827561 (hardcover) |
ISBN 9781459827578 (PDF) | ISBN 9781459827585 (EPUB)
Subjects: LCSH: Sharks—Juvenile literature.
Classification: LCC QL638.9 .L45 2022 | DDC j597.3—dc23

Library of Congress Control Number: 2021950059

Summary: This nonfiction book for middle-grade readers examines
the biology, habitat and mythology of, threats to and latest research
on sharks. It asks us to look at sharks as friends not foes.

Orca Book Publishers gratefully acknowledges the support
for its publishing programs provided by the following
agencies: the Government of Canada, the Canada Council
for the Arts and the Province of British Columbia through
the BC Arts Council and the Book Publishing Tax Credit.

Front cover photo by Michael Geyer/Getty Images
Back cover photo by Ken Kiefer 2/Getty Images
Author photo by Alex Waterhouse-Hayward
Design by Jenn Playford
Edited by Kirstie Hudson

Printed and bound in Canada.

25 24 23 22 • 1 2 3 4

Illustrated silhouettes of marine life under the waves.
SOLARSEVEN/SHUTTERSTOCK.COM

For Rob Stewart. Thank you for sharing your love of sharks with the world. This book, and millions of sharks swimming in the oceans today, would not be here without your passion. For all the young eco-heroes proving you are never too young to help save the planet. And for everyone doing what they can to save the sharks—which starts with finding out more about them. Since you're reading about sharks, that means this book is dedicated to you.

CONTENTS

FOREWORD

By Captain Paul Watson

***Sharks Forever!* I certainly do hope so. This diverse group** numbering some 500 species has been around for over 420 million years, yet many, if not most, of these amazing species could disappear within this century.

Humans have already wiped out 79 percent of sharks from the global seas with tens of millions being slaughtered every year.

We hear about the relatively few shark attacks every year but ignore the millions of sharks that die by human hands. We have created the myth of a monster thanks to irresponsible movies like *Jaws*, yet when all is said and done, it is we who are the real monsters.

The general view that sharks are dangerous has very little evidence to support it. In fact, it is safer to surf, swim and dive among sharks than it is to play golf—the number of people killed on the golf course by lightning strikes and bee stings is much higher than those killed by sharks. Hundreds of millions of people go into the ocean every year, yet the average number of people killed is about five. Dogs and horses kill many more people than sharks do.

And if people continue to be afraid of sharks, they should take the advice of legendary surfer Kelly Slater, who said, "If you're afraid of sharks, just stay out of the water."

The ocean, after all, is their home, not ours. Yet defending sharks is also a defense of our species.

Without the crucial ecological role that many species of sharks play, global oceanic marine ecosystems would be greatly harmed and diminished, with tragic consequences we have not yet fully considered but that would gravely impact humanity.

There have been milestones in shark-conservation efforts, and it has been my privilege to have worked with the late Rob Stewart to produce the widely acclaimed documentary film *Sharkwater* and to contribute now to promoting this book, *Sharks Forever,* by Mark Leiren-Young.

I have worked in the past with Mark, in connection with orcas, and I have witnessed that he possesses the three most important virtues of a conservation activist—passion, imagination and courage.

I have spent decades physically intervening against shark poachers, and these interventions have saved hundreds of thousands of sharks. While stopping the shark finners on the waters has been effective, I have come to understand over the years that to be truly successful, our actions must be accompanied by educating the public about how ecologically important sharks are, and how all of us have an obligation to do what we can to defend sharks and diversity and interdependence of all species in the sea.

These absolutely perfect creatures roamed the seas long before the dinosaurs. Sharks have survived the last four mass extinction events, but will they survive the sixth major extinction—the Anthropocene?

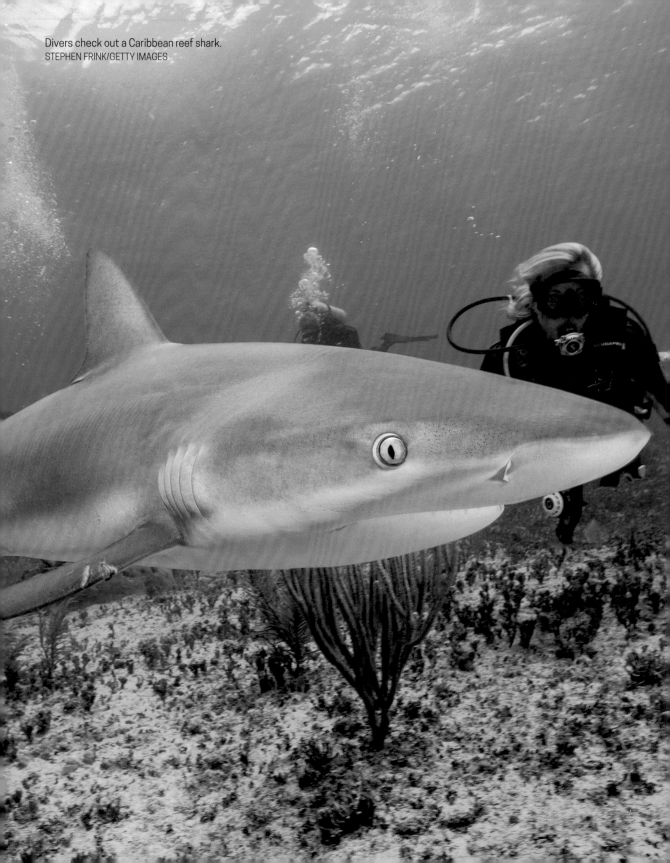

Divers check out a Caribbean reef shark.
STEPHEN FRINK/GETTY IMAGES

INTRODUCTION
Fear and Learning

"My goal is to make people fall in love with sharks. And for that, people need to see a bit of their softer side, a bit of their intelligence, and maybe see a bit of themselves in the sharks."

—Rob Stewart, filmaker and shark lover

A great white shark shows off some great white teeth.
ALESSANDRO DE MADDALENA

Sharks scared me. When I went to the Vancouver Aquarium as a kid, I thought rays looked sleek and sci-fi, like spaceships. The octopus was clearly an alien. Orcas, belugas and dolphins were adorable. Sharks looked like monsters. And that was before I saw the most terrifying movie of all time.

I was in high school when I saw *Jaws*. The slogan for the movie about an unstoppable great white shark was, "You'll never go in the water again." After seeing *Jaws*, I never wanted to. I had friends who were afraid to get into swimming pools, never mind rivers, lakes or shallow waters off beaches that no great white had ever seen.

I'd seen sharks in the wild too. Adults who took me fishing were furious when dogfish ate the bait on lines set to catch salmon. When I saw those small sharks hauled onto the deck of a boat, they looked fierce—even as they fought to stay alive.

I eventually got over my fear of going in the water, but I was still terrified of sharks. Then I met Rob Stewart at a film festival in Barcelona. Sharks never scared Rob. He was only nine the first time he met a shark and discovered the 5-foot (1.5-meter) reef shark was scared of him.

Rob set out to make a documentary to show people that sharks aren't monsters but rather a vital part of the world's ecosystem. And they need our help. After seeing his movie *Sharkwater*, in which Rob swims, plays and even cuddles with sharks, they no longer looked so scary to me. And they stopped looking quite so scary to people around the world. Rob's passion was contagious. People were inspired to help save the fish that so many had considered pests, competitors or monsters.

When I launched my podcast, *Skaana*, to share stories about the challenges facing orcas and oceans, one of the first people I planned to interview was Rob. Then he died in a scuba-diving accident. The next year I helped promote Rob's final movie, *Sharkwater Extinction*, to spread his message about saving sharks, oceans and humans—because we all need healthy oceans to survive.

I wrote this book to keep promoting that message. And to answer my own questions about sharks. I wanted to discover the history and mystery of these awesome, ancient animals, share their stories and—most of all—find out what we can do to keep our oceans full of sharks forever. So let's dive in.

Don't worry—nothing's going to bite.

Sharkwater filmmaker Rob Stewart.
SHARKWATER PRODUCTIONS

Whale sharks, rays and tuna at the
Okinawa Aquarium in Japan.

1
Love at First Bite

"I am a nice shark, not a mindless eating machine. If I am to change this image, I must first change myself. Fish are friends, not food."

—Bruce, the great white shark in *Finding Nemo*

A great white shark near Guadalupe Island in Mexico.
SHARKCREW/WIKIMEDIA COMMONS/CC BY-SA 4.0

Hunt
ILLUSTRATED BY SIE DOUGLAS-FISH

Sharks don't want to eat you. If you stop reading right now, you've already learned the most important thing that everyone should know about sharks.

If you swim in the ocean every day for 100 years, you are more likely to be struck by lightning than swallowed by a shark. Lightning kills more than 4,000 people a year. It is riskier to swim with another human than with a shark. Humans aren't just more likely to drown you—they're more likely to bite you.

The BBC reported in 2021 that snakes kill 138,000 people per year. Dogs kill almost 60,000 of us. Crocodiles kill 1,000 humans a year. Around 500 people a year are killed by hippos. So how many people are killed by sharks most years?

Five.

Meanwhile, humans kill at least 100 million sharks a year.

And we're scared of them?

A sand tiger shark goes to school in the Monitor National Marine Sanctuary off the coast of North Carolina.
GREG MCFALL, NOAA/FLICKR.COM/PUBLIC DOMAIN

SHARK BITES OR SHARK ACCIDENTS?

The International Shark Attack File (ISAF) found proof of only 470 fatal, unprovoked bites during the last 450 years. The ISAF researchers at the University of Florida—who study past and present records of sharks hurting humans—say there are about 80 unprovoked bites each year. Most happen in the waters near the United States and Australia.

Gavin Naylor, director of the Florida Program for Shark Research, told me that about one-third of all shark bites are what he considers "provoked." This doesn't mean humans were asking for it, but it does mean they were doing something that was definitely going to get a shark's attention. The incidents he considers "provoked" include people bitten while feeding sharks or spear-fishing—hunting in the water, surrounded by sharks. They also include people trying to be nice to sharks by freeing them from nets or trying to remove hooks from their mouths or bodies. I have a friend on Maui who rescued several sharks by freeing

A mako shark jumping for bait.
ALESSANDRO DE MADDALENA

Beware of shark! A warning sign for surfers and beachgoers on the west coast of Hawaii.
MATTHEW MICAH WRIGHT/GETTY IMAGES

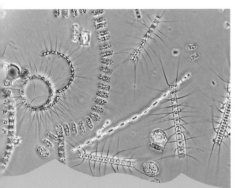

SHARK BITES
Plankton

Most types of plankton are tiny. There are two types of plankton. Phytoplankton are tiny plants known as algae. Zooplankton are animals, including tiny fish, krill and a lot of other species without backbones. *Plankton* comes from the Greek word for "drifter"— because these species don't swim but drift with the tides. Because nature is complicated, there are larger kinds of drifters, like some shellfish and jellyfish. So not all are small. Many marine animals, including the biggest sharks and whales in the sea, eat only plankton.

UNIVERSITY OF RHODE ISLAND/STEPHANIE ANDERSON/NASA EARTH EXPEDITIONS

them from sticks, hooks or fishing gear, and he was never hurt. But since a shark may not know you're trying to help, they're more likely to bite you than write a thank-you card. Swimming near sharks—or even surfing near them—isn't considered provoking them.

Australia frequently declares war on sharks. When a surfer or swimmer is injured by a shark, the Australian government responds like the shark is a human serial killer. The difference is, when the authorities claim they're hunting a specific shark who bit a human, they aren't looking for the "guilty" shark. They just kill sharks in the area to prove they're taking the bite seriously.

Between 2001 and 2017 more people in Australia were killed by kangaroos than by sharks. Authorities don't hunt killer kangaroos. Horses were involved in one-third of that country's animal-related human deaths. If Australian authorities treated horses the way they treat sharks, every time a horse killed a human they'd shoot every horse in the herd and every horse found anywhere near that herd.

BIG SHARKS, SMALL FOOD

Basking sharks look like they could devour you and your best friend for lunch, with room left over to swallow a hippo for dessert. They are the second-biggest fish in the sea. Only whale sharks are bigger. And they are absolutely deadly...to **plankton**. Unless you are a microscopic plant, fish or shellfish, a basking shark isn't going to eat you, even as a pizza topping.

If a whale shark or a basking shark spotted you, it is possible that you might interest them. You'd probably be the weirdest thing they'd seen in the water that week.

Maybe your puny human head looks as funny to them as a hammerhead's looks to you.

Great white sharks have plenty of teeth—about 240 at any time, set in five rows. The teeth are sharper than steak knives. These sharks aren't looking to eat people either.

No shark is.

All animals eat something to survive—except in cartoons. But most, if not all, incidents where sharks "attacked" humans were accidental.

How do we know this?

When a shark bites a human, they leave almost immediately to find real food. These bites are exploratory. Sharks don't have iPhone apps to identify other species, so they may bite a person to find out what they are and whether they'd make a decent dinner.

The ISAF records from 2020 show that over 60 percent of people bitten by sharks that year were surfing or boarding at the time. Surfers look like prey. Divers don't. Fewer than 10 percent of the people bitten by sharks were diving or snorkeling with them at the time. So people swimming with sharks are safer than people surfing near them. The ISAF has an interactive map that shows where bites have happened and what type of sharks were involved. On rare occasions, tiny cookiecutter sharks—who grow to only about 28 inches (71 centimeters)—take bites out of long-distance swimmers in Hawaii.

"Almost every animal is more dangerous than sharks," shark researcher Jim Abernethy told me. After spending most of his life swimming with sharks in Florida, Jim doesn't believe sharks ever hunt humans, because of how they behave after they bite people. "They're not actually

SHARKS!
Great Whites

The superstars of the shark world, the largest great whites are believed to grow to over 20 feet (6 meters) long. They usually swim 15 miles per hour (24 kilometers per hour), but they move faster when they're hunting. Great whites—most experts just call them whites—prefer the waters off South Africa, New Zealand, Australia and North America. Their sense of smell is like a superpower. They can smell food from over a mile away.

ALESSANDRO DE MADDALENA

Julia Barnes swims with a friendly nurse shark in Bimini, Bahamas.
KAREN BARNES

A great white shark breaches the water in South Africa.
ALESSANDRO DE MADDALENA

shark attacks. They're shark mistakes," says Jim. "Sharks bite and release everybody they bite."

KILLER KANGAROOS VERSUS KILLER SHARKS

Sharks taste humans the way baby humans taste sand and dirt. If one out of every thousand babies on earth ate a worm, would you declare that humans are worm-eaters?

Of more than 500 shark species, just three are responsible for the majority of cases where sharks were blamed for killing humans. According to the ISAF, great whites are at the top of the list for most fatal bites on record, followed by tiger sharks and bull sharks. Almost no other type of shark has ever killed a human. And saying all great whites, all tiger sharks or all bulls are dangerous to humans is the same as saying all dogs, horses and kangaroos are dangerous to humans.

Snorkeling with a whale shark in
Quintana Roo, Mexico.
KEN KIEFER 2/GETTY IMAGES

Because these three shark species have teeth with sharp edges that are used to cut and hold their prey, their bites tend to do more damage than the bites of other sharks. In recent years we've learned that great whites—and many other sharks—spend a lot of time closer to shore than anyone ever imagined. We've only discovered this due to tracking technology. If sharks thought people were prey, we would have noticed, because shark bites would happen every day.

A hammerhead hanging out near the ocean floor.
JULIA BARNES

IUCN RED LIST CATEGORIES AND CRITERIA, VERSION 3.1, SECOND EDITION

 **SHARK BITES**
Endangered, Extinct or Everywhere?

EXTINCT (EX)
No known living individuals

EXTINCT IN THE WILD (EW)
Known to survive only in captivity or as a naturalized population outside its historic range

CRITICALLY ENDANGERED (CR)
Extremely high risk of extinction in the wild

ENDANGERED (EN)
High risk of extinction in the wild

VULNERABLE (VU)
High risk of endangerment in the wild

NEAR THREATENED (NT)
Likely to become endangered in the near future

CONSERVATION DEPENDENT (CD)
Low risk; conserved to prevent being near threatened; certain events may lead to a higher risk level

LEAST CONCERN (LC)
Lowest risk

DATA DEFICIENT (DD)
Not enough data to make an assessment of the risk of extinction

NOT EVALUATED (NE)
Has not yet been evaluated against the criteria

A shortfin mako swims close to the surface
in Cape Point, South Africa.
ALESSANDRO DE MADDALENA

2
Inside the Shark

"Do you want to have a sea that's completely safe from sharks, or do you want to keep the sharks alive?"

—Alessandro De Maddalena, shark expert
and curator of a shark museum near
Cape Town, South Africa

A shark spine on the seashore at Sober Island, NS.
DENNIS JARVIS/FLICKR.COM/CC BY-SA 2.0

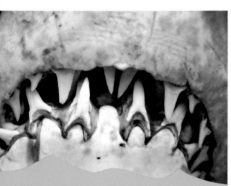

SHARK BITES
What Big Teeth You Have

Yes, shark teeth are sharp. If a front tooth is lost, a new tooth appears to replace it. We humans generally get 32 teeth throughout our lives. If there were a shark tooth fairy, they would have gone extinct—or at least broke—very quickly. Some of the biggest sharks may have more than 30,000 teeth in their lifetime—I've seen estimates that they may be able to have as many as 50,000. Sharks grow and lose teeth even before they're born. Even sharks in eggs have teeth!

ANDREW HOLT/GETTY IMAGES

Let's peek inside a shark and look beyond their impressive teeth. There are more than 500 types of sharks. Sharks live in every sea, many rivers and even some lakes.

Different kinds of sharks can be very different from one another. An adult megamouth's megasized mouth can be 4 feet (1.2 meters) wide. A dwarf lanternshark can swim in a soup tin!

There are several traits common to most types of sharks. Not only are baby sharks born with full sets of teeth, but they have teeth everywhere. Sort of. Sharkskin is rough because it's covered with tiny, sharp, toothlike scales called *denticles*. This rough skin provides protection from bites and helps sharks swim faster. Whale sharks even have denticles on their eyeballs!

Some sharks have denticles in their mouths. This skin is so rough that sharkskin has been used as sandpaper. In Japan, some sword grips are made with sharkskin.

Sharks don't have bones. They have *cartilage*. Cartilage is tough but flexible tissue that weighs less than bones. Weighing less helps sharks swim faster. Cartilage is also more flexible than bones. This allows sharks to make sharp, fast turns. The tip of your nose and your ears are made of cartilage.

HOW SHARKS SWIM

Most sharks swim by swinging their tails or moving their bodies from side to side. This movement pushes them forward. They can't swim backward.

Their famous *dorsal*—the pointy fin on their backs that is pretty much the universal symbol for sharks—also helps them balance and turn. Some sharks have vertebrae or backbones—a lot of them. A human has 33. A white shark has 133. This makes them very flexible.

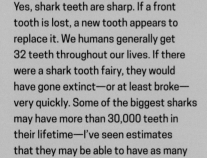

A shortfin mako shark.
NOAA/PUBLIC DOMAIN

The fastest sharks are really fast.

Shortfin mako sharks can swim 46 miles per hour (74 kilometers per hour). They can leap 30 feet (9 meters) into the air. Great whites can swim up to 35 mph (56 kph). Tiger sharks can swim 20 mph (32 kph). Olympic swimmers win medals moving about 6 mph (9.5 kph). Sharks can swim at full speed for only short bursts, so if you see them moving quickly, they're probably hunting.

Most sharks never stop moving, because they need to get oxygen through their gills. Gills are the small flaps on the sides of their heads that process oxygen from water. Different species have a different number of gills—seven, six or, most commonly, five. Sharks breathe in through their mouths and out through their gills. I was always told that sharks can't stop moving or they will die. This is sort

The gills of a great white shark.
ALESSANDRO DE MADDALENA/
SHUTTERSTOCK.COM

SHARK BITES
Ampullae of Lorenzini

Many sharks have electrical receptors in their jaws, heads and snouts (noses)—hammerheads have them in their big heads. These electrical receptors, called *ampullae*, are pores full of something that looks like jelly. Think shark zits. The receptors allow sharks to sense prey nearby even if that prey is staying still or hiding. They also allow sharks to tune in to the earth's magnetic field—which is how they navigate the oceans. **Ampullae of Lorenzini** are named after scientist Stefano Lorenzini, who discovered them in 1678.

ALBERT KOK/SCIENCE LEARNING HUB/CC BY-SA 3.0

of true. Some sharks have to keep swimming to get oxygen because it's the motion that pushes water through their gills. This is called ram breathing.

Many sharks have a small opening behind their eyes that helps them breathe when they're on the seabed or buried in sand. These special gills are called **spiracles**, and they allow sharks to stay still.

LIVERS, LORENZINI AND LATERAL LINES

The shark's liver helps them float. It is filled with fats and oils, which is one reason humans used to hunt sharks. A white's liver can make up more than a third of the shark's weight. Before humans drilled for oil, we used oil from sharks and whales as fuel. A study in 2020 suggested that shark oil could be used as biodiesel—a kind of fuel that people consider environmentally friendly. Does anyone really want to drive a car powered by hammerheads?

The gray nurse shark goes by many names, such as a sand tiger shark, a spotted ragged-tooth shark or a blue-nurse sand tiger.
MARTIN FISCH/FLICKR.COM/CC BY-SA 2.0

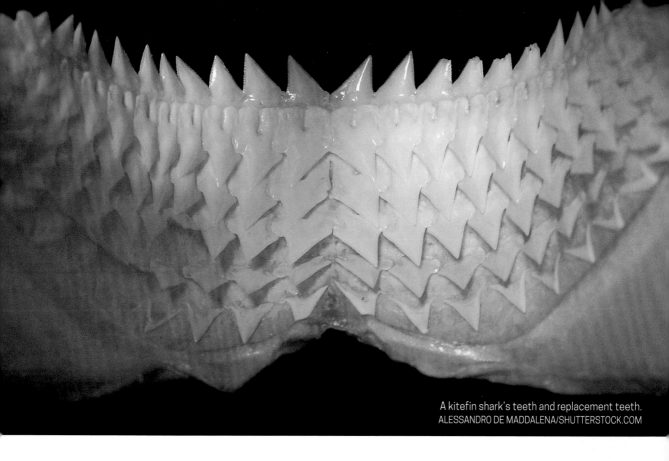

A kitefin shark's teeth and replacement teeth.
ALESSANDRO DE MADDALENA/SHUTTERSTOCK.COM

People used to believe sharks went crazy if they smelled blood. Some sharks can and do smell blood. Some can smell it from miles away. But it's not blood that sharks react to when they approach humans—it's people's movement or fear.

Most sharks have the ability to sense electrical currents. Because muscles—including hearts—emit electrical currents, it's impossible for their prey to hide. A shark's built-in electricity sensors are called ampullae of Lorenzini. Sharks also feel pressure and vibrations in the water, which also helps them detect prey. Organs known as *lateral lines* give sharks a supercharged sense of touch—they feel things without touching them.

People used to believe sharks never sleep. This is because they aren't built to close their eyes or even blink. Some

A shark-tooth necklace made with teeth from shark fossils.
CLIFF HUTSON/FLICKR.COM/CC BY-SA 2.0

A baby leopard shark before being released back into the ocean.
MOONJAZZ/WIKIMEDIA COMMONS/CC BY-SA 2.0

sharks have protective eyelids, or **nictitating membranes**, that cover their eyeballs when they're eating or fighting. Great whites and other sharks can flip their eyes inward to keep them from being injured by prey.

SHARK FARTS

Sand tiger sharks have a unique method of swimming. They pass gas! Sand tigers gulp air, hold it in their stomachs and slowly fart the air out as they dive. This lets them stay still at the depth where they want to hang out. Sand tigers are found in most oceans. They are considered a vulnerable species.

BABY SHARKS

In music videos baby sharks are adorable. But being a **baby shark** isn't easy. In many species, once a shark pup is born Mom is rarely around long enough to sing "Doo, doo, doo, doo, doo, doo" before swimming away. Moms leave quickly. This is a good thing, since the change in their body chemistry that stops them from seeing their babies as food doesn't last long.

Baby sharks have to learn to look after themselves—fast! One reason we use the word *shark* to refer to people who are ruthless is that in some shark species, such as sand tigers, the stronger babies eat weaker siblings in the womb or before they emerge from their eggs.

Female sharks tend to be larger and have tougher skin than males—sometimes three times as thick—because they're often injured by males when mating. Males frequently bite the females they're mating with. Male sharks have hooks called claspers to pin females when they mate. Babies in the same litter may have different fathers. Shark species reproduce in very different ways. Some sharks give birth to live young. Some sharks, like gray bamboos, lay eggs.

Undersea action! This group is swimming off the coast of Oahu, HI.
JAKOB OWENS/UNSPLASH

Rob Stewart swimming with Caribbean reef sharks in the Bahamas.
SHARKWATER PRODUCTIONS

3
Shark Brains

"There is no such thing as dangerous sharks, but dangerous situations...Once mankind can get rid of its fear from sharks, then sharks can be protected."

—Erich Ritter, shark expert

SHARK BITES
Filter Feeders

Instead of using teeth, **filter feeders** have pads that filter the seawater they swallow and bounce plankton toward their throats. These sharks suck in the water and keep the best plankton, and the rest of the water goes out through the gills.

How smart is a shark? A shark isn't likely to beat you on a science test. If one ever does, you really need to spend more time on your homework. But you're unlikely to beat a shark at tracking a school of fish. Sharks don't have a language—as far as we know. They don't make noise except by slapping water. The only sharks who have vocal cords are the ones in movies. The sharks in *Finding Nemo* talk, and the shark in *Jaws* growls. So how do real sharks communicate with one another?

They use body language, movement and slaps.

Are sharks psychic? Shark researcher Erich Ritter wondered if sharks might use some kind of ability we haven't discovered yet to share information at a distance. He found that easier to believe than the notion that

A gray reef shark at Kingman Reef in the Line Islands.

sharks, in over 400 million years, never developed any way to communicate with one another. He felt this ability explained why sharks would arrive for food—or steer clear of threats—despite being too far apart to see signals from one another. Shark researchers who have removed hooks from sharks have had other sharks who'd never seen them before swim to them for help. How did they know that these humans were helpful?

However sharks think, the size of their brains compared to the rest of their bodies is just as big as the brains of some shark-sized mammals. So if you're heard that sharks are mindless, they're not. People who study sharks or spend a lot of time around them agree that they are intelligent, curious and have distinct personalities and preferences.

SHARKS!
Megamouth Sharks

The megamouth sounds and looks mythical. The species was first spotted by scientists in Hawaiian waters in 1976, when an adult male died after getting tangled in the sea anchor of a Navy ship. The biggest megamouth seen so far is 16 feet (almost 5 meters) long, making this one of the largest sharks out there. Like whale sharks and basking sharks, megamouths are filter feeders. They're also not fast swimmers—with such big mouths to catch plankton, there's no need to swim quickly. These sharks have been found in oceans around the world but are rarely seen so no one knows how many there are.

A tiger shark about to snack on an albatross.
ILANA NIMZ, NOAA/FLICKR.COM/PUBLIC DOMAIN

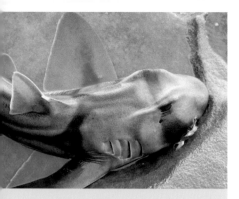

A Port Jackson shark.
PHOTOGENICCREATIVITY/FLICKR.COM/
CC BY-SA 2.0

SHARKS!

Gray Bamboo Sharks

Gray bamboo sharks live mostly in the Pacific Ocean but are also found in rivers and lagoons. They have brown or whitish underbellies. Their young have bands that disappear as the sharks get older. They aren't very active and tend to hang out at the bottom of water bodies, near sand, rocks, coral and mud. Fave foods are fish, shrimps, worms, mollusks and crabs. Gray bamboos can grow to a length of 30 inches (76 centimeters). They are classified as near threatened.

GERARD SOURY/GETTY IMAGES

SHARK MEMORIES

They say an elephant never forgets, but what about sharks?

Studying shark thinking is a challenge, because we don't know how a shark's brain processes information or memories. In 2015 biologist Vera Schluessel taught gray bamboo sharks to recognize shapes. And the sharks could still remember those shapes a year later. She also proved that sharks could learn to find their way through a maze. Her tests showed that the sharks could recognize optical illusions—the kind that often fool humans.

Found in the Pacific, gray bamboo sharks can grow to over two feet (just over half a meter) and, like great whites, often find their food partly by seeing it. A term for this is *visual feeder*. Her work suggests that visual feeders—which include great whites—could have great memories.

Sharks going to school—and schools going to sharks.
KELVIN GOROSPE, NOAA/NMFS/PACIFIC ISLANDS
FISHERIES SCIENCE CENTER BLOG/CC BY-SA 2.0

FISH AND MARSHMALLOWS

About 50 years ago, researchers invented a test to see how old a child had to be before they were willing and able to wait for a reward. Kids were offered one marshmallow and told that if they waited to eat it, they would get a second one. Kids started passing the test at age four.

Since then researchers have tried this kind of test on other animals. Smarter ones like crows and chimps pass this test too. In 2021 scientists in England proved that cuttlefish—very small fish who look like little squid—have self-control and understand the idea of the future. Since cuttlefish aren't fans of marshmallows, they were tested with live grass shrimp. If cuttlefish can pass this test, it's likely that a mako or a tiger shark can too.

A cookiecutter shark from the Gulf of Mexico. This small shark is named for the unique circular bites they take out of prey. PERSONNEL OF NOAA SHIP PISCES/ FLICKR.COM/CC BY-SA 2.0

SHARK BITES
Sharks and Rays

Rays are related to sharks. They are both in the group **Chondrichthyes**—fish with skeletons made of cartilage, not bones. There are more than 1,000 types of Chondrichthyans, including ratfish (chimaeras). When you see stories about shark populations, they are often referred to as "sharks and rays." Most bony fish have a swim bladder—an organ that contains gas to control how they float. Sharks don't have this organ. They use the oil in their livers—along with their fins—to control how deep they dive and how long they can stay down. Rays move their **pectoral** fins when they swim. Sharks don't. Rays, skates, penguins and sea turtles basically fly through the water by flapping their pectorals! Just because they're relatives doesn't mean they're friends. Hammerheads are big fans of snacking on stingrays.

CHEN MIN CHUN/SHUTTERSTOCK.COM

Fish freedom at the Monitor National Marine Sanctuary off the coast of North Carolina.
JOE HOYT, NOAA/FLICKR.COM/PUBLIC DOMAIN

4
New Old Sharks

"When it comes to sharks, the golden age of scientific discovery has just begun."

—Juliet Eilperin in her book *Demon Fish: Travels Through the Hidden World of Sharks*

SHARKS!

Land Sharks

Okay, I know I've told you not to be afraid of sharks, but there is one type of shark I'd be freaked out to meet. Walking sharks! Epaulette sharks (who look kind of like eels) use their fins to crawl on reefs at low tide and eat crabs and mollusks. In 2020 scientists found four new types of sharks near Australia and New Guinea who walk on land.

Can you imagine a vegetarian shark? For the bonnethead—who swims off the waters of Mexico, Brazil, Florida and California—fish may be friends, not food. These sharks—whose heads look a bit like the hammer-head's—not only eat their vegetables but also prefer seagrass to sea snails and shrimp! Bonnetheads grow to 30 to 48 inches (76 to 122 centimeters) long, weigh up to 24 pounds (11 kilograms) and are the first sharks to be officially classified as omnivores (eaters of plants and animals), not carnivores (animal eaters). Scientists discovered the bonnethead diet only recently, in 2021.

We learn new things about sharks all the time. In the 1980s, experts believed there were around 250 species of sharks. Today we know there are more than 500. One of the most exciting things about being a shark researcher is that there is so much to discover.

In 2019 smalltooth sawfish sharks were discovered off the waters of Indonesia. Sawfish are currently the most endangered species of sharks and rays.

A bonnethead shark, also known as a shovelhead shark, swimming in tropical waters.
WRANGEL/GETTY IMAGES

SHARKS WHO GLOW IN THE DARK

In 2021 scientists learned that three deep sea species of sharks are bioluminescent, which means they produce their own light. Researchers already knew that lanternsharks do this with **photophores** (organs that emit light)—it's how the species got its cool name. The surprise was that kitefin sharks—who grow to six feet (just under two meters)—also glow in the dark. The blackbelly lanternshark and the southern lanternshark don't just glow—they radiate light. Their bellies emit light, which allows them to see the prey below them. Their dorsal fins glow too. As I write this, kitefins are the largest known vertebrates (animals with backbones) who produce light. The oceans are vast, but technology is allowing us to go deeper than ever before, and scientists are paying more attention to sharks than ever before, so it's likely there are all sorts of amazing sharks we haven't met yet.

SHARK BITES
Shark GPS

How can sharks travel over 10,000 miles (16,000 kilometers) to precise locations? We've recently learned that sharks have better GPS than an iPhone. Sharks don't just sense electricity—they sense Earth's electromagnetic fields. The fields are created by metals in the earth's core and cover the planet. In 2021 scientists proved that sharks use their ampullae of Lorenzini to follow Earth's electromagnetic fields and find their way around the planet. The scientists created an electric field off the coast of Florida and tested 20 bonnetheads, confirming that the sharks could follow it.

A thresher shark swimming in the Philippines.
BEARACREATIVE/SHUTTERSTOCK.COM

A whale shark under the waves.
JULIA BARNES

THRESHER SHARKS

Thresher sharks' tails are as long as their bodies. Scientists recently discovered that they hunt with their tails, slapping their prey to stun or kill them. Thresher males are larger than females—they can be up to 25 feet (7.6 meters) long, compared to 18 feet (5.5 meters) for females. They live in tropical and cold waters around the world—in the oceans and near coasts. Some types of threshers are classified as vulnerable, while others are threatened.

SHARKS AS MEDICINE

A myth as deadly to sharks as the idea that they want to eat us is that sharks don't get sick. Scientists have recently busted this myth. Sadly, sharks get the same diseases we do. But because some people don't believe this, sharks are hunted for their organs, which are used to create "miracle" cures. These cures cost sharks their lives and aren't saving ours. Various parts of the shark are used as medicine. Beliefs about which pieces help human health differ between cultures. Shark cartilage is sold as a cure for arthritis everywhere and is probably in your local drugstore.

Fortunately for humans, and unfortunately for sharks, the oil from some sharks does have confirmed medicinal value. The oil *squalene*, which helps sharks swim, increases the power of vaccines in humans. It was first used in flu shots in 1997. When humans were rushing to create a COVID-19 vaccine in 2020, some people raised concerns that this was bad news for sharks. Shark hunters might have used medicinal use to justify increasing their catches, but they would have been lying.

In 2020 more than three million sharks were hunted and killed for their oil. But very little of their oil is needed or used for medicine. Ninety-nine percent of shark squalene is sold for use in sunscreen and moisturizer. Endangered sharks aren't being killed to save lives—they're being killed to make skin cream.

Squalene doesn't have to come from sharks. It is also found in plants like sugarcane and olives. This is a new discovery. Even though it takes more than 2,500 sharks to produce a ton of squalene, some people still consider it easier to take the oil from sharks than from plants. But the more we learn about sharks, the fewer excuses there are to kill them.

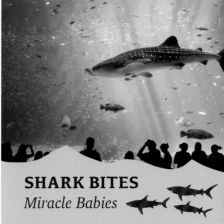

SHARK BITES
Miracle Babies

One shocking new discovery is that female sharks can reproduce without males. Several aquariums reported babies showing up in tanks full of female sharks who hadn't encountered males in years— or ever. This is even more proof that sharks are the ultimate survivor.

Bottles of shark cartilage on sale.

A 922-pound (418-kilogram) thresher shark in New Zealand.
ARCHIVES NEW ZEALAND/WIKIMEDIA COMMONS/CC BY-SA 2.0

5
Sweet Lemon Sharks

"We understand marine mammals much better than we understand sharks because we knew that they have similar brain structures compared to us. The whole shark-behavior field is new and exciting."

—Shark Lab scientist Félicie Dhellemmes

Félicie Dhellemmes with her friendly neighborhood lemon shark.
CHELLE BLAIS

PETRI BELLONII CENOMANI
Κύων καρχαρίας, Canis carcharias : Noruagi Perlzfilch.

LIBELLA.

Zigænam Græci, Libellam Latini vocauerunt, fabrorú lignariorum & architectorum inftrum
tum, è quo dependente perpendiculo, rectas parietum ac lignorum facies oculorú nixu pernofc
cui inftrumento quòd is pifcis(cuius hic picturam vides)veluti adamuffim refpondeat, Oppian

French naturalist Pierre Belon's woodcut illustration from 1553 of a shark he named Canis carcharias.
BIODIVERSITYLIBRARY.ORG, PUBLIC DOMAIN

Sharks have friends? Scientists at the Bimini Biological Field Station in the Bahamas—known as Shark Lab—have discovered that sharks have friends. People used to believe all sharks were loners. Félicie Dhellemmes is a behavioral ecologist who studies what animals do and how they do it. She says personality studies on sharks are a 21st-century phenomenon.

Until recently shark studies were mostly done on dead sharks. Today we've gone from dissecting their bodies to trying to understand their minds.

Scientists at Shark Lab study young lemon sharks. Lemon sharks get their name from their lemony color. They're good sharks to study because they spend the first few years of their lives living in shallow waters near the roots of mangrove trees. This allows them to hide from larger sharks. They can also survive out of water for a couple of minutes, which makes it easier for scientists to tag and work with them.

A lemon shark with a sweet personality.
CHELLE BLAIS

Félicie wasn't surprised to learn that sharks have distinct personalities, because we now know that many species—even ants—have personalities. Some young sharks are explorers who leave their *nursery*. Others are shy and stick to familiar mangroves. Félicie was fascinated to discover that sharks not only have personalities but also the sense to adjust their behavior and become less playful when sharks looking to eat them are nearby.

Young lemons are very social and hang out in same-sex groups. They learn hunting techniques and about their environment from their friends. Félicie says her team doesn't know if the sharks are related. If they were, it would be interesting to discover that sharks have family bonds, given that mothers leave their pups at birth.

Australian researchers have learned that their country's Port Jackson sharks choose specific Port Jackson sharks to hang out with. And nurse sharks sleep in groups of up to 40—cuddled together on the ocean floor.

SHARK BITES
Who or What Is a Shark?

In 2021 environmental leaders, including Jane Goodall, asked newspapers around the world to stop writing about animals like they are things. They asked reporters to start referring to any animal they write about as a who, not a what. That's what I do in this book. I won't refer to an animal as it or that—which is still the way most people write and talk about animals.

SHARK BITES
San Jose Sharks

The San Jose Sharks can be a pretty scary hockey team, depending on the season—and not just because their stars often favor the longest, weirdest beards of any hockey players. The above photo is my brother, David Young, wearing a San Jose Sharks jersey.

COURTESY OF MARK LEIREN-YOUNG

A large group of gray reef sharks in French Polynesia.
TOMAS KOTOUC/SHUTTERSTOCK.COM

ANTHROPODENIAL AND SHARK FRIENDS

Humans aren't keen on admitting that any other animal might be like us in any way. Claiming an animal might love or laugh or feel sad is known as anthropomorphizing, which means thinking an animal or thing experiences the world the way people do. It's the only scientific concept I've come across that doesn't seem to have any scientific evidence behind it. Some animals, such as orcas, elephants and apes, have the same brain cells that allow humans to have complex emotions. Brain cells called spindle neurons process emotions like love and embarrassment.

Scientists used to claim that animals couldn't feel pain. I was told this when I went fishing and watched adults not just catch salmon and sharks but also smash their heads in with bats. I was probably six or seven the first time I saw it, and I was sure the grown-ups were lying to me. They may have been lying, but it was what scientists told them before a study in 2018. And this isn't just about scientists not thinking fish could feel pain. Until 1980 many scientists didn't believe human babies could feel pain! They were convinced we didn't develop pain receptors until we were about a year old. Some scientists believed this until 1999. OUCH!

Because anthropomorphism is considered unscientific, some scientists invent complicated terms to avoid admitting an animal is doing something that seems human. When people tickle monkeys and they laugh, these scientists call the laughter "tickle-induced vocalizations." That term is silly enough to make me laugh.

When a study in 2020 showed that gray reef sharks hang out with the same groups—as human friends do—the director of the study called these sharks "associates." Scientist Yannis Papastamatiou told a journalist,

"They are not friends in the sense of having any emotional bond with each other." While his study may have proved that the sharks hang out with the same groups, it did not test for or prove that they don't have emotional bonds.

In 2001 Dutch scientist Frans de Waal came up with a term for people who claim animals don't have feelings, emotions or intelligence. His term is my favorite word—*anthropodenial*. He defined it as "a blindness to the human-like characteristics of other animals, or the animal-like characteristics of ourselves." I anthropomorphize. A lot. And I think those gray sharks who hang out together are friends. Do you?

Rob Stewart enjoying a free dive with reef sharks in the Bahamas.
VERUSCHKA MATCHETT/
SHARKWATER PRODUCTIONS

SHARKS!

Reef Sharks

Reef sharks swim near, you guessed it, reefs. Both are found in tropical waters, such as off the coasts of Australia. As the top or **apex predators** in their neighborhoods, reef sharks are essential to the health of a reef ecosystem. Apex predators prevent other species from overwhelming—and overhunting—an environment. In the same way that wolves in land areas prevent grazing animals from eating too many plants, sharks help control their ecosystems. Reef sharks are hunted for their flesh and fins and are often caught accidentally by people fishing for other species. They are also a top tourist attraction. Research keeps showing that this makes live reef sharks much more important to a country's economy than dead ones.

The Bahamas and Honduras outlawed longline fishing in 1993 and made all forms of shark hunting illegal in 2011. People there didn't have a tradition of hunting sharks, but shark hunters from around the world showed up in their waters. Almost half the divers who visit these places hope to dive with sharks. A study in 2020 that looked at 371 reefs in 58 countries found that nearly 20 percent no longer had sharks. There are many species of reef shark, and as a group they are classified as near threatened.

KRISTINA VACKOVA/SHUTTERSTOCK.COM

A whale shark in Mexico feeds near the surface.
MATTHEW T RADER, MATTHEWTRADER.COM/
WIKIMEDIA COMMONS/CC BY-SA 4.0

6
Swimming with Sharks

"This species is always the monster in every story. But in mine, they were siblings. Their presence was my happy place and their disappearance was my call to action."

—Madison Stewart, Shark Girl

Julia Barnes on a boat in Bimini, Bahamas.
KAREN BARNES

If you've ever wondered whether individual sharks have personalities, Julia Barnes says you just need to hang out with enough sharks. "Some are bold and will bump cameras, checking you out. Others are shy and stay their distance."

Julia fell in love with sharks after watching *Sharkwater* when she was 12. During a dive in the Bahamas when she was 17, Julia went underwater with a diver who was an experienced shark feeder. She was 60 feet (18 meters) underwater when she found herself surrounded by about 30 reef sharks. Many were longer than she is tall—and she's 5 feet 11 (180 centimeters)! "One shark swam over me, rubbing his belly against the top of my head. Others flicked my face with their fins." She said the sharks took turns eating and seemed almost polite about it. This isn't the way sharks behave in movies, where food almost always drives them crazy.

Julia Barnes hanging out with a hammerhead.
KAREN BARNES

Julia filmed those sharks for a movie she made to help save the oceans, called *Sea of Life.* She says blue sharks—and others—are interested in cameras because their ampullae of Lorenzini react to electronic gear. A baby mako about 24 inches (61 centimeters) long was very curious about her and her camera. "She munched on my GoPro. She was the most adorable little shark I'd ever met."

Her favorite sharks are great hammerheads, which grow up to 20 feet (6 meters) long. "Their personalities are awesome. They are shy and curious at the same time." During a visit to Bimini in the Bahamas, there were two great hammerheads on the surface and several nurse sharks about 20 feet (6 meters) below her. Julia went free diving—diving without air tanks—so she could film them.

The hammerheads swam close to the surface several times to check her out. Then a nurse shark surfaced to watch her. "The nurse shark got so close I felt like she wanted something," says Julia. "I reached out my hand and touched her head. She slowed down, seemingly enjoying being pet." The shark's skin was bright and sparkly, covered with brown dots.

SHARK GIRL AND CHEEKY SHARKS

Madison Stewart, known as Shark Girl because of her work fighting for sharks in Australia, loves swimming with sharks. She was living on a boat in Australia with her parents when she was two. Her family often explored the Great Barrier Reef. She started diving at the reef when she was 12. At 14, Madison realized the sharks were disappearing. She dropped out of school, started homeschooling and set out to save the sharks as a filmmaker and activist.

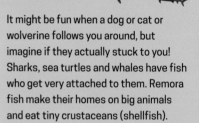

SHARK BITES
Remoras

It might be fun when a dog or cat or wolverine follows you around, but imagine if they actually stuck to you! Sharks, sea turtles and whales have fish who get very attached to them. Remora fish make their homes on big animals and eat tiny crustaceans (shellfish). Some even clean their host's teeth. Yes, some sharks have personal, tiny dental hygienists.

Madison Stewart, also known as Shark Girl.
SHARKWATER PRODUCTIONS

Madison Stewart making friends
with a shark.
JUAN MEDINA

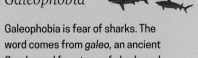

SHARK BITES
Galeophobia

Galeophobia is fear of sharks. The
word comes from *galeo*, an ancient
Greek word for a type of shark, and
phobia, which means "fear." If you let
people know that sharks don't want to
eat them, you can help cure galeophobia.

When Madison was young, her dad was more concerned
about her riding a bike than swimming with sharks.

Madison has met mellow sharks and "cheeky" sharks.
She told me her favorites are tigers, which she and others
call the great whites of the tropics. "They are the only
sharks I see that display both perfection and grace, as well
as clumsiness and character." There is a small great white
in south Australia whom dive operators named Pip. That's
Madison's other nickname. "She's aggressive with a lot of
attitude," says Madison. "Fitting."

DEEP BLUE

One of the stars of the shark world is Deep Blue. This
female great white is the biggest great white ever
photographed by scientists—so far. She's about 20 feet
(6 meters) long and is likely more than 50 years old.
Deep Blue was first spotted in waters near Mexico in the
1990s. The first research footage of her was taken in 2013.

In 2019 marine biologist Ocean Ramsey, who started swimming with sharks when she was 14, swam with her near Hawaii. That same year Deep Blue was spotted sharing a sperm-whale feast with two other female whites. We've recently learned that whites from different parts of the world don't pal around when they meet. Whites from North America won't swim with whites from South Africa and Australia. Do they have different accents or attitudes or body language? We don't know. Yet.

A smooth lanternshark from the Gulf of Mexico. These small sharks are only slightly longer than a pencil!
SEFSC PASCAGOULA LABORATORY; COLLECTION OF BRANDI NOBLE, NOAA/NMFS/SEFSC/ WIKIMEDIA COMMONS/PUBLIC DOMAIN

EMMA

Jim Abernethy, who runs ecotours, writes books and makes movies about sharks, told me his favorite sharks are tigers. "If you look at their characters by species, the tiger shark is clearly the most curious and the most playful—kind of like the Labrador retriever." That's not exactly the reputation these sharks have among people who hunt them.

In 2002 Jim was in the waters near his Florida home when he saw a 9-foot (2.7-meter), one-eyed lemon shark with a hook through his jaw. "I came up with this crazy idea. I wondered if I could make friends with the shark, like I would a strange dog, by giving it love and affection." About two hours later, the shark allowed him to get close enough to remove the hook. Jim has been removing hooks from sharks ever since. "I went on a mission to make friends with every shark and remove all their hooks." Jim earns their trust carefully and gradually. He has a hand signal to invite sharks over for head rubs or hook removal.

Around 2001 Jim met a tiger shark at Tiger Beach in the Bahamas nicknamed Emma. She's boss tiger—when Emma shows up, other tigers make room for her. She is also a sucker for head rubs—at least from Jim.

SHARKS!

Canada's Sharks

Porbeagles are known as Canada's sharks since up to 90 percent of porbeagles are found in Canadian waters, mostly in the North Atlantic. They grow to almost 10 feet (3 meters) in length and prefer their water cold. Like a lot of cold-water sea life, porbeagles can live a long time—about 46 years. But there aren't a lot of them. In 1961 Canada had a porbeagle fishery that—along with Norwegian longline fishers—almost wiped out the species before the fishery was closed in 2013. Porbeagles were hunted for their meat and fins (think shark-fin soup) and for such things as fertilizer. They are among the fastest fish in the ocean. There is no evidence of a porbeagle ever biting a human.

Julia visits with a hammerhead.
The shark's remora tags along.
JULIA BARNES

A mosaic from Pompeii at Naples National
Archaeological Museum.
NAPLES NATIONAL ARCHAEOLOGICAL
MUSEUM/CC BY-SA 2.0

Since meeting Emma, Jim has removed four hooks from her body. "When you take a constant pain away from an animal, you become an instant friend." When they're both in the water, Emma follows Jim around. Since Tiger Beach is a popular place for shark tours, Emma is likely the world's most photographed shark.

Does Emma love Jim? Does she consider him a friend?

We don't know what emotions sharks can feel—but we never really know what anyone else is feeling, whether they're a shark or a human.

And just because sharks don't bite people the way we've been told they do, doesn't mean it's a good idea to try touching random sharks.

A tiger shark swims along a plant-covered
seabed in the Bahamas.
IMAGE SOURCE/GETTY IMAGES

A bull shark checks out the photographer.
UME-Y/FLICKR.COM/CC BY-SA 2.0

7
The Biggest Fish in the Sea

"The ocean is a place of paradoxes. It is the home of the great white shark, two-thousand-pound killer of the seas. And of the hundred-foot blue whale, the largest animal that ever lived. It is also the home of living things so small that your two hands may scoop up as many of them as there are stars in the Milky Way."

—Rachel Carson, environmentalist, from her book *Under the Sea-Wind*

A diver swims with a whale shark in Indonesia.
TORSTENVELDEN/GETTY IMAGES

Whale sharks are so big they seem impossible. Imagine a shark the size of a school bus. Whale sharks have a flat head, a pair of dorsals near the rear of their body, a gigantic tail and really cool sparkly spots. They aren't called whale sharks because they're whales but because they are *huge*. They can grow up to 40 feet (12 meters) and weigh more than 40 tons (36 metric tons). Their mouths can be 4 feet (1.2 meters) wide. They are the biggest fish in the world and bigger than almost any other living being on the planet.

The blue whale and fin whale are bigger than whale sharks—but they're mammals, not fish. The giant squid can also grow to be bigger than a whale shark. This makes it easy to believe that legendary monsters called kraken really existed.

It takes time to grow so big. Whale sharks can live longer than a century, possibly even 150 years. Perhaps in clean water with plenty of prey, and without being bothered too much by us, they can live longer. It takes a lot of food to keep a whale shark moving. A whale shark spends about eight hours a day eating. A healthy whale shark eats more than 45 pounds (20 kilograms) of plankton a day.

SWIMMING WITH WHALE SHARKS

Adult whale sharks often feed at the surface of the water, but they can dive as deep as 328 feet (100 meters). Researchers and tourists often chase them because whale sharks are harmless to humans. They might accidentally bump a person, but they don't bite us. They can't. So that makes them safe to swim near—and study.

Some people even hold their fins. Researchers know what they're doing and may do this for useful reasons. If someone who isn't studying sharks is touching one,

SHARK BITES
Shark Week versus Sharks?

The myth that sharks want to hurt humans is killing sharks. The tens of thousands of shark encounters each day that end with sharks ignoring people don't make the news. But anytime someone is bitten by a shark, claims to have been bitten or even sees a shark and gets scared, it's reported all over the world. I know—shark stories are cool. That's why you're reading this. But shark experts worry that the amount of attention sharks get every time they're spotted in "the wrong place" may be fatal. Shark expert Alessandro De Maddalena says many people believe there are more sharks in the oceans than ever before. Why? Because shark stories are always in the news. Discovery Channel has Shark Week just once a year. But in the news media and on social media, every week is shark week.

SHARKS!

Dwarf Lanternsharks

The tiniest sharks in the world are dwarf lanternsharks. They are found in the waters of the Caribbean. Like other kinds of lanternsharks, they have their own built-in light sources. They have glowing photophores (organs that emit light) on their stomachs and fins. Many lanternsharks also have sharp quills on their dorsal fin spines. They are listed in the "data deficient" category. There is a species known as green lanternsharks. As far as we know, their only superpower is bioluminescence (the ability to emit light). Dwarf lanternsharks live deep in the Atlantic—1,440 feet (439 meters) down. They eat squid and octopuses.

A basking shark shows off a big mouth.

please don't encourage them by liking their images on social media.

These sharks have over 300 rows of teeth. Their teeth are at the mouth rim and are used not for chewing food but for trapping it. They are filter feeders and every four hours these huge fish can filter enough seawater to fill an Olympic-sized swimming pool.

Whale sharks like to travel. Slowly. They swim about 15 miles (24 kilometers) per hour. While they often live solo, they do sometimes meet in large groups. People have seen hundreds of these sharks meeting one another. Whale sharks are found in most tropical seas.

Female whale sharks don't start giving birth until they are around 30 years old. They give birth to live young who are just over one and a half feet (about half a meter) long. But as I'm writing this, in 2021, scientists don't know where the moms give birth. We rarely see baby whale sharks.

BASKING SHARKS

Basking basically means hanging out in a pleasant place. You know the old guy sleeping on a large floating air mattress in the pool? He's basking.

I live in Canada, on Vancouver Island. My province, British Columbia, is home to a lot of environmental leaders. That doesn't mean we are or have always been environmentally friendly. Before I was born, basking sharks were easy to find off the BC coast. Today they are almost never seen near BC.

What happened?

In 1949 the Government of Canada declared basking sharks "destructive pests." Were they destructive to us?

Nope. These 20- to 26-foot (6- to 8-meter), 11,000-pound (4,989-kilogram) sharks are filter feeders. They hang out at the surface of the water, slurping plankton. So unless you're plankton, you're safe from them.

Even though basking sharks don't hurt humans, they are fatal to fishing nets. When the sharks were getting tangled in nets and ruining them, the people running fishing boats complained. The government came up with a solution. They attached a blade to a fisheries patrol boat. The people who protect humans on the water were ordered to ram basking sharks and kill them.

If anyone thought this was a bad idea, newspapers at the time didn't report it. The Canadian Coast Guard killed more than 400 basking sharks in BC waters. They didn't do anything with the bodies except let them sink. News stories about the hunts made the men who killed the sharks sound like heroes. Fishers killed others, often shooting them for fun. Today if someone sees a basking shark near BC, it's a cause for celebration. It only happens about three times a year.

Basking sharks are endangered in some parts of the world because they are slow-moving and so easy to catch.

SHARK BITES
Shark Whiskers

Some sharks—like bullheads—have something that looks like a cat's whiskers. They're called *barbels* and can be used to sense prey—and, I guess, if one fell in the water, cats.

A gray reef shark in the Pacific Remote Islands.

A great white shark breaks the surface to reach for bait in South Africa.
BERNARD DUPONT/FLICKR.COM/CC BY-SA 2.0

8
Megalodons and Ancient Sharks

"Man versus meg
isn't a fight,
it's a slaughter."

—Jonas Taylor, from the science fiction movie *The Meg*

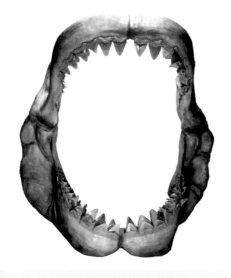

The jaws of a megalodon are estimated to have spanned 6.6 feet (2 meters) across.
CHIP CLARK, USNM PAL 537883, SMITHSONIAN INSTITUTION

Megalodons are mind-boggling. Today these ancient sharks are superstars. Movies have always loved big monsters like Godzilla and King Kong. How could screenwriters resist when scientists discovered there was once a shark who made great whites look like goldfish? If you like dinosaurs, how can you not love megalodons? Movies like *The Meg* imagine what it would be like if a megalodon showed up today looking for lunch. In this kind of movie, sharks don't bite humans by accident.

Megalodon remains are found all over the world, including in North America, South America, Europe and Africa. These ocean giants could grow to about 60 feet (18 meters) in length. This is about twice the size of a whale shark. Scientists believe these giants were wiped out about 3.6 million years ago. So unless someone invents

A megalodon and an orca.
ILLUSTRATED BY SIE DOUGLAS FISH

Jurassic Park technology, you're never likely to meet a megalodon. To get a sense of just how long a megalodon is from tip to tail, picture an adult giraffe standing on the head of another adult giraffe, who's balancing on the head of a third adult giraffe.

GLORIOUS SHARKS!

The name megalodon comes from ancient Greek and means "big tooth." The full scientific name is *Carcharocles megalodon*, which is Greek for "big-toothed glorious shark." Those big teeth were 3.5 inches (9 centimeters) long. The biggest meg tooth found (so far) is over 7 inches (18 centimeters) and was discovered in South Carolina in 2021. They aren't just the largest sharks we know of— they're one of the largest animals period. Scientists think these massive sharks could live almost 100 years. A megalodon's bite was more powerful than any other animal's, including *Tyrannosaurus rex*. Imagine a megalodon fighting a *T. rex*. I'd watch that movie!

When I talk about whales, I've been asked, "Who would win? A killer whale or a megalodon?" I always say orcas, because brains and strategy can almost always beat size and strength. But megalodons were really big, so if I were an orca, I'd steer clear of that fight. Mind you, some orcas like to snack on great white sharks because they think their livers are tasty, so who knows?

THE OLDEST FISH IN THE SEA

Greenland sharks hang around the waters of the Arctic and North Atlantic Oceans near—spoiler alert—Greenland. The longest-lived human we know of survived 122 years. Scientists recently discovered that Greenland sharks can

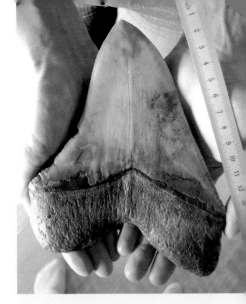

The size of a fossilized megalodon tooth compared to a hand. This one is 7 inches (18 centimeters) long, measured diagonally.
LONFAT/WIKIMEDIA COMMONS/PUBLIC DOMAIN

SHARK BITES
Baby Megalodon...
Doo, Doo, Doo,
Doo, Doo, Doo, Doo

Megalodons gave birth to and raised their young near shallow shorelines. These areas are known as shark nurseries. When they were born, baby megalodons were about 6.6 feet (2 meters) long—tall enough for careers in pro basketball.

SHARK BITES
The First Shark?

One of the earliest sharks who looked pretty much like sharks today was *Cladoselache*. Fossil records show that they lived around 380 million years ago. Unlike today's sharks, they had seven gills. Most sharks today have five. They were also long—almost 6.6 feet (2 meters)—but not muscular. These shark ancestors didn't have denticles. Their skin was soft. One of the earliest and best shark fossils, a specimen of *Doliodus problematicus*, was found in New Brunswick in 1997 and is about 400 million years old. Because cartilage doesn't last long, scientists learn about ancient sharks by studying teeth, fins, spines and scales.

live for over 400 years, maybe even 500. We know how old they can get only because scientists are studying Greenland sharks who have been accidentally caught by fishing crews.

These sharks were swimming in the Arctic and North Atlantic Oceans before Shakespeare started wearing diapers, never mind writing plays. If you think school is lasting forever, consider this: Greenland sharks don't hit their teens until they're about 150 years old. They are the fifth-biggest sharks. They can grow as long as 21 feet (6.4 meters) and weigh 2,200 pounds (1,000 kilograms). They live in cold places, so they have a very slow metabolism. (Metabolism is the rate at which your body turns food into energy.) It's not just their metabolisms that are slow. These sharks move verrrrrry slowly. They usually swim about 0.76 miles (1.2 kilometers) per hour.

Greenland sharks are not considered harmful to humans. The only known report of a possible attack on a person from a Greenland shark was in 1859.
DOTTED ZEBRA/ALAMY STOCK PHOTO

A Greenland shark (slowly) swimming through cold waters near Nunavut.
HEMMING1952/WIKIMEDIA COMMONS/CC BY-SA 4.0

They aren't fussy eaters and will take their food dead or alive. And they eat everything from polar bears to reindeer.

One reason these sharks survive so long may be that not many people live as far north as they do, so few humans ever hunted them. Even if they had, they wouldn't have wanted to take a bite. This shark's flesh is poisonous unless it's specially prepared. The chemicals in their bodies include a unique shark antifreeze that allows them to survive in the Arctic. They swim in water as cold as 30 degrees Fahrenheit (-1 degree Celsius). Their shark antifreeze is toxic to humans and other animals. In Iceland, Greenland shark bodies are hung for five to six months to remove the toxin before being prepared as hákarl or kæstur hákarl—the national dish.

Sharks, as a group, have been here for about 455 million years. That means sharks were here before people, before birds and about 200 million years before dinosaurs. Sharks haven't just been on earth much longer than humans. They've been here longer than trees.

SHARKS!

Frilled Sharks

Frilled sharks look so prehistoric that some people call them living fossils. They grow to about 7 feet (2.1 meters) in length. They live in oceans around the world, but they're almost never seen because they live on the ocean floor. They look and move like eels. Frilled sharks have 25 rows of long teeth. Each tooth has three points. These sharks also have denticles in their mouths. The three-pronged teeth make it easier for them to catch their fave food—slippery squid. Their name comes from their unique gills, which cover their necks like frills. Scientists think frilled shark pregnancies are longer than that of any other species on earth—possibly up to 42 months. The species is considered threatened.

CITRON/WIKIMEDIA COMMONS/CC BY-SA 3.0

Cage divers checking out a couple of great
whites as the sharks check out the divers.
STEFAN PIRCHER/SHUTTERSTOCK.COM

9
Great White Lies

"Why do I love great white sharks? It's like you're seeing a god of the ocean."

—Alessandro De Maddalena, shark expert

This photo from the 1870s shows men measuring sharks and other sea life. SMITHSONIAN INSTITUTION ARCHIVES, ACC. 11-006, BOX 002, IMAGE NO. MAH-1630

SHARKS!

Great White Baby Sharks

A great white pregnancy lasts almost a year. Females give birth to two to four live babies at a time. Many species of sharks—including great whites—have areas scientists call nurseries, where they give birth and then leave or raise their young. One great white shark nursery was discovered around 2016, near Long Island, New York. The not-quite-great-yet white sharks don't leave home until about age 20. For the first few years of their lives, whites eat fish. When they're older, they switch to larger prey. The fave food for whites is seals. Great white sharks can live to be about 75 years old.

Jaws almost ended sharks. When *Jaws* was released in 1975, it was one of the most popular movies ever—the first-ever summer smash hit. There was no social media, but *Jaws* made news everywhere. Not only were there sequels, but suddenly there were all sorts of movies about killer sharks. The real damage *Jaws* did to sharks by turning them into the stuff of nightmares was creating a media feeding frenzy that hasn't stopped since 1975. Any shark bite anywhere—and every shark sighting near a beach—is reported as if sharks declared war on swimmers or surfers.

Sailors have been wary of sharks for centuries. But the rest of the world? Not so much. Most people never thought about sharks. And when people did talk about sharks they weren't always considered scary.

American businessman Hermann Oelrichs was so sure no shark had ever bitten a human that in 1891 he put up a cash prize for anyone who could prove they had. When he saw a shark, Hermann jumped into the water to prove his point. The shark swam away, like sharks usually do. Many people back then thought stories of sharks attacking humans were fish tales. And if sharks were a threat, it was only to fishers. But that was before people around the world started to think it was fun to vacation on the beach, and surfing became a sport.

JERSEY SHORE SHARKS

In 1916 five people were bitten by a shark, or sharks, off the shores of New Jersey. Four of them died. The incidents took place over about two weeks. This was long before the internet, long before television news, but the story still went viral. People were so doubtful sharks could do this, they originally suspected that sea turtles had bitten the humans!

When an 8-foot (2.4-meter) great white shark with a stomach full of pieces of people was caught near New Jersey, everyone assumed this was the killer. No one knows if that shark killed anyone or just ate the people after they were dead. But this was the original killer great white. Experts still aren't sure if the shark—or sharks—responsible for the deaths were great whites or bull sharks.

The New Jersey incidents inspired what became known as "rogue shark theory." Australian scientist Victor Coppleson came up with the term. He also wrote a book called *Shark Attack* and claimed "rogue" sharks had developed a taste for eating humans. What used to be called shark bites suddenly became known as shark attacks.

SHARK BITES
Sharknados

Jaws isn't the only movie that features sharks as monsters. In the world of sci-fi there are shark-like villains in the *Star Wars* universe. In the *Sharknado* movies, sharks get caught in tornadoes and fly at their victims. DC Comics has a shark who walks on land. King Shark fights superheroes like The Flash and is super evolved. Played by Sylvester Stallone in the movie *Suicide Squad*, King Shark is still not evolved enough to be nice. He can talk, is huge and has deadly teeth. As you can see when he eats police officers, King Shark is not a filter feeder.

A shark caught on a longline.
WAYNE HOGGARD, NOAA/NMFS/
SEFSC/FLICKR.COM/CC BY 2.0

THE MYTHS OF SHARK WEEK

Jaws writer Peter Benchley said the New Jersey events didn't inspire his book or screenplay—but a couple of other real events did. In 1971 the documentary *Blue Water, White Death* showed a great white who looked determined to snack on the filmmaker in a diving cage. Of course, the people making the movie were feeding the shark at the time. The images were terrifying. They were perfect for a horror movie.

In *Jaws*, the captain of the boat chasing the monster shark tells a story about his ship being sunk and his being stranded in the water for four days as sharks attacked his drowning friends. This story was based on an incident in World War II. The USS *Indianapolis* was torpedoed by a Japanese submarine. At least 300 men died when the ship went down. About 800 sailors tried to keep afloat—with and without life jackets—for four days before rescuers arrived.

Sharks definitely circled the survivors, but they were also circling hundreds of dead bodies, wounded sailors and all the food that had spilled from the ship. It is likely that

A shark smiles for the camera while checking out cage divers.
BERNARD DUPONT/FLICKR.COM/CC BY-SA 2.0

A great white shark saying hello to divers in a cage in Australia.
ALESSANDRO DE MADDALENA

with no access to help and with the sailors fighting exhaustion and dehydration, any bite would have been fatal. A Discovery Channel Shark Week documentary called this "the worst shark attack in history." There are claims that as many as 150 men were killed by sharks, likely whitetips and tigers. As far as I can tell, this number is based on… wanting to make it sound very scary. No one knows how many sailors died because of shark bites or how many died of dehydration, starvation or exhaustion. That's why this horrible incident is not included in the International Shark Attack File's official records of shark-related deaths.

Thanks to *Jaws*, great white sharks became the most famous—and feared—animals in the world. We know great whites are smart, because they are able to catch and eat some of the smartest animals in the seas, including seals and dolphins. Researchers who study them say whites sometimes hunt cooperatively, working together like orcas and wolves do. They will also breach—jump up out of the water—to stun their prey. The only animals who hunt whites are orcas and humans.

HUMANS AGAINST NATURE

People who hunt for "sport" often chase animals known for their deadly skills as predators. These hunters want to boast about killing animals who are capable of killing them. In Africa, the lion, leopard, rhino, elephant and buffalo were considered "the big five" by trophy hunters. Hunters who wanted to show off their skills were determined to kill at least one of each. Wherever humans live, trophy hunters—who like to pretend it's a fair fight when they chase unarmed animals with expensive, fancy weapons—attack the local apex predators.

JULIA BARNES

SHARK BITES
Yum-Yum Yellow

If you're planning to go into the water and are worried about a shark wanting to taste-test you, here's some advice from the International Shark Attack File experts. They suggest wearing darker colors, because sharks see high-contrast colors really well. So the bright yellow that we use to help rescuers spot us may attract sharks. Some researchers joke that for sharks, the color of life jackets and life rafts is "yum-yum yellow." This is also why you should cover your dive watch and avoid wearing shiny jewelry in the water. Sharks tend to steer clear of groups, so it's best not to swim alone. Don't splash much. Sharks are also most likely to be hunting and hungry at twilight or after dark. And, yes, if you're bleeding, stay out of the ocean. If a shark does approach you to bite, hit it on the nose, ideally with something solid. This will usually convince the shark that you're too much trouble to bother with. Sharks also steer clear of sea snakes, so some shark experts wear striped wet suits that make them look like sea snakes.

Researchers measuring a tiger shark during an annual shark survey.
JEREMY ADAMS, NOAA

Sportfishers tend to have a better reputation than hunters. This may be because most humans aren't emotionally attached to fish. It's also because people who hunt big, fast fish often eat them. Yes, you may still see huge trophy fish stuffed and mounted on walls, but the fish were likely dinner first. Not many hunters eat lions, tigers or bears. Some sportfishers are keen on chasing fast fish like marlin and makos. Others get their kicks chasing the deadliest fish—which is bad news for great whites.

From the moment *Jaws* debuted, great white sharks became the planet's most feared predator. This turned sharks into the ultimate trophy for some sportfishers, who wanted to prove they could kill these deadly beasts. This is kind of ironic, because the shark in *Jaws* was almost impossible to catch and kill, but that story was fiction. Whites are easy to catch, because they're not afraid of boats or humans.

A great white breaches in South Africa.
ALESSANDRO DE MADDALENA

Sportfishers aren't as bad for sharks as industrial fishing operations are. There aren't that many people chasing sharks for fun. They don't catch anywhere near as many sharks as industrial fishers. But they are chasing and killing the biggest, oldest, healthiest sharks out there.

Years after the movie based on his book was one of the biggest hits in the world, Peter Benchley said that in a new version of *Jaws*, the shark wouldn't be the monster. "The shark in an updated *Jaws* could not be the villain; it would have to be written as the victim, for, worldwide, sharks are much more the oppressed than the oppressors."

The poster for Sharkwater Extinction.
SHARKWATER PRODUCTIONS

10
Sharkwater

"When it came to animals, the closest
I could get in all my imaginings
to hunting alongside a dinosaur or
riding on the back of a dragon was
swimming with sharks."

—Rob Stewart

SHARK BITES
Longlines

In longline fishing, long wires with anywhere from 25 to 2,500 baited hooks are strung out in the water to catch fish. The lines may be miles long, and they can be set on the ocean floor or at the surface. They don't just catch the fish they're looking for—they also kill anything that takes their bait, including turtles, birds and dolphins. This method of industrial fishing is only slightly less horrifying than trawling, where fishing boats drag huge nets through the water, catching everything in their path. Imagine if ranchers herded cows by chasing them with bulldozers.

Dried shark fins for soup.

Rob Stewart rewrote *Jaws* with humans as the monsters and sharks as the victims. The Canadian environmentalist was 22 when he set out to film sharks and tell their stories. He was inspired after discovering, to his horror, that sharks were being killed by industrial fishing boats in the Galapagos Marine Reserve.

If sharks weren't safe in the Galapagos—one of the world's most famous marine protected areas—where were they safe?

The answer? Pretty much nowhere.

In *Sharkwater*, which was released in 2006, Rob swam with sharks. He also made friends with them. He didn't just live to tell about it but also showed the world these famous fish weren't mindless killing machines.

Rob met Captain Paul Watson, founder of Sea Shepherd, and joined him on a mission to fight illegal shark fishing. His movie let the world know that illegal fisheries existed. Rob filmed poachers off the shores of Guatemala attacking the Sea Shepherd boat. He also risked his life to film sharks being illegally killed for their flesh and fins (for food for humans and animals).

SOUP VERSUS SHARKS

Over 100 million sharks are hunted and killed each year—many of them just for their fins. This is because in some Asian cultures shark-fin soup is a delicacy and a sign of wealth. It can be very expensive, which means fins are a pricy item. One pound of dried shark fin can cost more than $300 US.

Fin soup goes back to the Song dynasty (960–1279). Other fancy foods at the time included bear paws, camel humps and monkey brains. None of those are still popular menu items today. Shark soup seemed to stick around because it became a traditional part of celebrations like weddings. Or maybe shark fins—which are very bland—are still tastier than monkey brains?

In the finning industry, fishers often catch these sharks, slice off their fins and throw the dying, bleeding sharks back into the water to drown. Even in the brutal world of industrial fishing, finning is shockingly cruel. Celebrity chef Gordon Ramsay called finning "the worst act of animal cruelty I've ever seen." Imagine how people would react if a hunter cut off a giraffe's legs and left her in the forest to die.

SHARKWATER VERSUS SHARK-FIN SOUP

When Rob discovered that the taste for shark-fin soup helped drive illegal shark hunts, he was determined to have his movie shown in China. The Chinese government refused to allow it because officials took offense to certain scenes. Rob cut some footage from *Sharkwater* and added scenes of Chinese basketball superstar Yao Ming asking people to stop serving and eating shark-fin soup. The revised movie was shown in China in theaters and on TV.

A bowl of shark-fin soup.
ANDREW CURRIE/FLICKR.COM/CC BY-SA 2.0

Cuts of fish meat at a market in Malaysia.
JOHN/FLICKR.COM/CC BY-SA 2.0

Shark meat at an outdoor fish market in Dubai.
PAUL FENWICK/FLICKR.COM/CC BY-SA 2.0

SHARKS!

Scalloped Hammerheads

Rob's favorite shark was the scalloped hammerhead, which he considered the coolest animal on earth. Hammerheads have 360-degree vision. They can see and feel you everywhere. Scalloped hammerheads are so named because of indentations, or scallops, in the middle of their uniquely shaped heads. They can use their dorsal fins to swim on their sides. Rob loved swimming with them. Scalloped hammerheads enjoy swimming with one another. They swim in large groups—which makes them easier to catch than most sharks. Males grow to about 5.9 feet (1.8 meters) and weigh about 64 pounds (29 kilograms). Females have been known to grow to 14 feet (4.3 meters).

Great hammerheads can grow to be over 13 feet (4 meters) long and 3 feet (0.9 meters) wide and can weigh more than 1,000 pounds (454 kilograms). They can and do swim in shallow warm water, because that's where they find their fave food—rays. They are known to use their wild heads to pin those rays down.

In 2014 scalloped hammerheads became the first species of shark to be protected by the US Endangered Species Act. They are critically endangered, but are still caught by Australia's commercial fisheries.

SHARKWATER PRODUCTIONS

Rob believed that if the world knew the stupid reasons sharks were being killed, people would rally to save them. He set out to discover why the oceans were losing millions of sharks each year beyond the ones being caught by legal fisheries.

Rob proved that illegal fisheries are a multibillion-dollar business. He also revealed that millions of sharks are killed by accident—possibly as many as 50 million each year. These sharks are caught and killed by industrial fisheries hunting for tuna and other fish.

Rob drowned in a diving accident in 2017. He was using special new gear designed to disturb the water as little as possible. Why? He wanted to get as close as possible to the sharks he loved without scaring them.

ROB'S MOVIES

Rob made three movies that helped change the world for sharks and humans. *Sharkwater* was released in 2006. At a screening of *Sharkwater*, Rob was asked why he was bothering to save sharks if the oceans were dying. This inspired his next movie, *Revolution*. *Sharkwater Extinction*, which exposed the illegal fish trade, was finished after Rob's death and released in 2018.

There is an award for young filmmakers in Rob's name. His family and friends run the Rob Stewart Sharkwater Foundation to help support ocean conservation through awareness, education and entertainment. The Canadian Screen Award for best science or nature documentary or program is given in his name. In 2018 a new species of deepwater cat shark was discovered in the Indian Ocean and named after Rob—*Bythaelurus stewarti*.

Rob Stewart filming a ham shark—okay, a hammy shark who clearly wants to be in his movie!
SHARKWATER PRODUCTIONS

SHARK BITES
Rob's Law

Canadian Member of Parliament Fin Donnelly, who helped pass Canada's anti-finning law in 2019, credited Rob as his inspiration. Finning became illegal in Canada in 1994, but buying and selling fins was still legal. Canada's anti-finning law makes it illegal to import or export shark fins—although that doesn't make it impossible to find shark-fin soup in Canada. Canada was the first country in the G20 (a group of the world's 20 wealthiest nations) to pass this kind of law. More than 90 countries around the world have banned shark finning. But almost no countries have banned importing fins. And as long as there's a market for fins, sharks will be caught for their fins. The anti-finning law also requires consideration of Indigenous Knowledge and encourages Indigenous Peoples to be part of policy development, monitoring and fish habitat decisions.

ED DUNENS/FLICKR.COM/CC BY-SA 2.0

Reef sharks hanging out near a coral reef.
NATURE, UNDERWATER AND ART PHOTOS/
NARCHUK.COM/GETTY IMAGES

11
Humans versus Sharks

"Sharks are beautiful animals, and if you're lucky enough to see lots of them, that means that you're in a healthy ocean. You should be afraid if you are in the ocean and don't see sharks."

—Sylvia Earle, world's foremost ocean expert

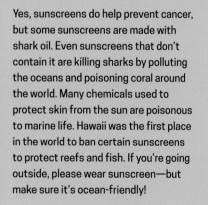

CORAL KILLING
SUNSCREENS

OXYBENZONE OCTINOXATE OCTOCRYLENE HOMOSALATE

ENZACAMENE PABA PARABENS TRICLOSAN

ANY
NANOPARTICLES

ANY FORM OF
MICROPLASTIC

SHARK BITES

*Sunscreen versus
Coral Reefs*

Yes, sunscreens do help prevent cancer,
but some sunscreens are made with
shark oil. Even sunscreens that don't
contain it are killing sharks by polluting
the oceans and poisoning coral around
the world. Many chemicals used to
protect skin from the sun are poisonous
to marine life. Hawaii was the first place
in the world to ban certain sunscreens
to protect reefs and fish. If you're going
outside, please wear sunscreen—but
make sure it's ocean-friendly!

Sharks have to deal with the same problems facing the planet that we do. They also have to deal with us. The issues threatening the earth are ones we created and keep creating. Penguins aren't polluting with plastics. Foxes aren't burning fossil fuels. Chimps aren't causing climate change. Yes, cow farts aren't helping—but we're the species packing cows onto industrial feed lots. Wild cows aren't farting away the ozone layer. Yes, this is the really depressing part of our story. But if you're reading this, you probably already know we need to treat the planet better.

BYCATCH

Bycatch is a harmless-sounding word that makes the slaughter of millions of animals sound like no big deal. This is the term used to excuse catching and, generally, killing anything other than what you are officially fishing for. So if you're fishing for tuna and accidentally kill sharks, birds or other species, they're known as bycatch. So many animals are being killed "by accident"—accidents that could be avoided if industrial fishing practices were outlawed, changed or even properly policed—that some animals will become extinct due to bycatch. Some may have already become extinct thanks to it. In 2016 *National Geographic* reported that one-third of what tuna fisheries caught using longlines wasn't tuna—it was sharks, rays and turtles. Accidental captures are also the biggest threat to such species as sea turtles and some whales.

MERCURY RISING

Mercury is released from coal-burning power plants and factories and, like almost all trash, eventually ends up in the oceans. The problem is not just that mercury poisons fish but that it also makes those fish poisonous. If you are eating shark, you are eating mercury and other heavy metals that cause all sorts of diseases. One of the many ways pollution affects marine life is by raising mercury levels. The bigger and older the fish, the higher their mercury levels. The higher your meal is on the food chain, the more toxic it is. So big fish—like sharks, marlin and tuna—are higher in mercury.

ORCAS EATING GREAT WHITES

In Africa some people are trying to blame orcas for scaring great white sharks away. There are exactly two orcas who are into shark hunting—Port and Starboard. The two sharks have figured out that if they flip a white shark over,

Tuna on sale in Japan's Tsukiji Market, considered the world's largest fish market.
SEAN PAVONE/SHUTTERSTOCK.COM

SHARKS!

Tuna

Sharks are not tuna, but a lot of sharks are caught by people fishing for tuna. The tuna industry was once infamous for catching and killing dolphins, who like to swim with tuna. Since humans are big fans of dolphins, when this made the news people—especially young people—stopped eating tuna. Tuna hunters quickly changed the way they fished—or claimed to change the way they fished. An environmental organization labeled tuna from these fishing boats dolphin-friendly.

This does not mean the tuna fisheries are also shark-friendly or that there is no other bycatch. Sadly, it doesn't always mean they are dolphin-friendly either. Regulating the fishing industry doesn't do much if no one enforces the regulations. Most boats fishing for tuna—or anything else—don't have anyone on board to make sure rules are being followed. The way we know most "dolphin-safe" tuna is dolphin-safe is because the captain of the ship says it is. What could possibly go wrong? And this is the world of legal fishing.

A lot of fish around the world are caught illegally. And as the tastiest tuna becomes scarcer, it becomes more expensive. In 2019, a Japanese restaurant paid $3.1 million US for a single 612-pound (278-kilogram) bluefin tuna.

JSEGALEXPLORE/SHUTTERSTOCK.COM

A fishing boat with a couple of painted sharks leading the hunt.
ANDREW MOORE/FLICKR.COM/CC BY-SA 2.0

it is unable to move and makes for a fine snack. Alessandro De Maddalena doesn't believe for a moment that two clever orcas have done more damage to the great white population than humans have. He runs a shark museum near Cape Town, South Africa, and he's convinced that most reports on the status of marine life are impossible to trust because they're based on the idea that people hunting fish will report their own crimes. Alessandro, and many of the shark lovers I spoke to who are fighting to save sharks and oceans, think we should end fishing—at least for a while.

Alessandro says we need to stop all fishing activities for 10 years to help the fish and the seas recover. He wants to find other work for people who fish, because he's not convinced there is what governments and industries call a "*sustainable* catch." Julia Barnes also wants people to stop fishing. Madison Stewart wants to end fishing too. So does Captain Paul Watson. They all say killing sharks destroys marine ecosystems because sharks keep other populations in check.

They also want to remind people that eating apex predators like sharks is about as healthy as smoking. This doesn't surprise me. For six years I lived on Maui.

A whitetip shark scoping a reef in Hawaii.
JOHN BURNS/NOAA, 2017/FLICKR.
COM/PUBLIC DOMAIN

One thing I loved about my Hawaiian home was eating fish that was local and even, sometimes, caught by friends. I ate a popular local dish, ahi poke, almost every day with a side of fresh papaya or pineapple. I couldn't imagine a healthier meal. I was in the best shape of my life…until I started feeling tired. My doctor asked what I was eating. When I boasted about all my ahi lunches, he was horrified. He ran a test and discovered my mercury levels were off the charts. My poke had poisoned me. It took me years to recover.

Mercury attacks our nervous system and kidneys. Because mercury can do irreversible damage to a developing brain, it's especially dangerous to children and pregnant or nursing mothers. Governments around the world urge people to seriously limit their intake of some types of tuna, shark, swordfish and several other species. In Canada the limit for most adults is about 5 ounces (142 grams) per week. To give you an idea of how small that amount is, consider that a McDonald's Quarter Pounder patty is 4 ounces (113 grams) before it's cooked.

Some doctors say that women who are pregnant, nursing or planning to become pregnant within a year should completely avoid several kinds of large fish, including shark, swordfish, ahi tuna and bigeye tuna. Even if you're not giving up fish, scientists and governments around the world are warning us to avoid eating too much big fish—including canned tuna.

AND THEN THERE'S PLASTIC

When most people imagine plastic pollution in the ocean, they picture fish caught in the rings from tins or that famous turtle in Costa Rica with a straw stuck up his nose. Yes, please, stop using single-use plastics. But most

SHARK BITES
Do You Eat Shark?

Shark is sold around the world with all sorts of unsharky names. English names used to sell shark to people who might not be keen on buying or eating shark—or feeding it to their cats—include cape steak, gummy, ocean fish, ocean filet, rigg, rock salmon, sea ham, huss, dogfish, catfish, grayfish, steakfish, whitefish and lemon fish. If someone offered you rock salmon, would you think it was shark? Fish is regularly misidentified—often on purpose to sell it for higher prices. A Canadian study showed that almost half of all fish sold in Canada isn't accurately identified. Shark shows up in a lot of North American cat food, often as ocean whitefish.

Healthy tuna?
MIKE MOZART/FLICKR.COM/CC BY-SA 2.0

Here I am posing with a model shark after the Vancouver Canucks hockey team (which has an orca symbol on its logo) beat the San Jose Sharks in a playoff game.
RAYNE ELLYCRYS BENU

of the plastic poisoning the oceans isn't from your lunch leftovers. It's not even from the world's top plastic-waste producers. Yes, I'm talking to you, Coke, Pepsi and Nestlé! The reality is that almost half the plastic in the oceans is waste from industrial fishing.

While all plastic eventually breaks down, it doesn't disappear. It is eaten, though. Fish mistake plastic bags for jellyfish. And filter-feeding sharks and baleen whales weren't built to strain out plastic.

Large pieces of plastic shrink, and some plastic starts out small. All of it eventually ends up in pieces so small they're called microplastics, and pretty much everything in the oceans eats them. In 2020 almost 70 percent of sharks in the waters near the United Kingdom had eaten—and contained—microplastics. The United Nations estimates that 100,000 marine mammals a year are killed by plastic pollution. If we keep polluting at current rates, the plastic in the oceans will outweigh fish in the oceans by 2050. If you are what you eat, you're part plastic—because every animal on earth is eating it.

Plastic pollution on display in the Royal BC Museum's exhibit *Orcas: Our Shared Future*.
SHANE LIGHTER, ROYAL BC MUSEUM

A great white shark breaches to catch a seal-shaped decoy.
ALESSANDRO DE MADDALENA/SHUTTERSTOCK.COM

A shark hanging out at home in the Great Barrier Reef.
JEFF HUNTER/GETTY IMAGES

12
Sharks and You

"Everyone can change the world. Saving the world doesn't have to be complicated. Just take what you love and what you're best at, smash them together and create for yourself a life of purpose and meaning. Not only will your life not be boring—your choice will inspire others to do the same."

—Rob Stewart

Sharks can recover. Oceans can recover. The planet can recover. The good news is that marine ecosystems have an almost miraculous ability to regenerate. The bad news? It only happens if we leave them alone.

Rob once told me the best hope for the sharks is *you*. He was convinced young people would understand that the fight for other species is essential. When I hosted an event for him in Vancouver, Rob told the audience, "Every revolution in the past has been led by the people most directly influenced by the atrocity, and right now kids are going, 'You guys have taken that. That's ours.'" This was about 10 years before Greta Thunberg began carrying a protest sign to raise awareness about climate change.

PEOPLE FOR SHARKS!

When I meet young people fighting for the oceans, Rob's name comes up all the time. Madison Stewart was featured in Rob's last movie, *Sharkwater Extinction*. She helped him

Rob Stewart filming a closeup of a friendly shark for his movie *Sharkwater Extinction*.
SHARKWATER PRODUCTIONS

show how sharks are abused by the commercial fishing industry and sportfishers. "Rob was my hero," she told me, "and, in the end, like a brother to me."

She originally set out to stop shark fishing around the Great Barrier Reef—an area that's crucial to the global ecosystem. When she starred in *Shark Girl*, Madison discovered that only one-third of the reef was off-limits to commercial fishing. Fishers were allowed to catch 80,000 sharks per year. This was despite research showing that several sharks there were on the verge of extinction and despite the fact that, as apex predators, sharks are essential to keeping the reefs healthy. Today, she says, there is still only a tiny part of the Great Barrier Reef where shark fishing is not allowed. "The area is also not significantly large enough to cover the home range of reef sharks—so it basically offers them no protection."

Madison fights to raise awareness that shark is sold in stores and restaurants in Australia and England as flake. At 24 she was named Australian Geographic Society's Young Conservationist of the Year. She has filmed Australian fishery officials killing sharks and was threatened with criminal charges if she shared the footage. She did. She wasn't charged.

Madison wants to find new jobs for people who fish for a living. In 2018 she visited Indonesia to meet and find out more about the people who catch sharks. After that she launched Project Hiu, a nonprofit organization that helps Indonesians switch from hunting sharks to showing them off to tourists. *Hiu* is the Indonesian word for "shark." Madison says she doesn't have hope for the oceans because "hope is a surrender. You shouldn't have hope when you can actually do something about it."

SHARKS!
Shark and Chips

Flake is often the fish in fish and chips in Australia and England. Most people don't realize that flake is shark. Letting people know what they're really eating could help save sharks! Madison Stewart says several fish-and-chip shops took shark off their menus after she shared facts with them about sharks and mercury.

MARAZEM/DREAMSTIME.COM

SHARK BITES
Sharks as Family

Some human societies who live near sharks see them as guides, gods or family. They are seen as powerful, not evil. The Japanese have a shark god of storms. Hawaiians consider sharks family and guardians. Hawaiian cultures share different stories of a being who is half shark, half human. Indigenous Peoples living on New Ireland island in Papua New Guinea know sharks so well that they have "shark callers" who summon them with traditional songs and rattles made of bamboo and coconut shells. They catch them by hand. Their culture and way of life is now being threatened by overfishing and commercial fisheries.

Above and below: Shark activist Ella Grace checking out the water.
KATE GRACE

BEAUTIFUL SHARKS

Twelve-year-old Canadian ocean activist Ella Grace says being surrounded by about 20 sharks when she was diving in Florida was "probably the best moment of my entire life." Ella fell for sharks when she was four years old and saw *Sharkwater*. "That movie put me on my path." She watched *Sharkwater* the way some kids endlessly watch Pixar movies. She figures she'd seen *Sharkwater* 300 times by the time she was seven, which was when she gave her first speech for Sea Shepherd. In 2019, when she was nine, Ella went from her home in Toronto to Bimini to swim with sharks. She was surrounded by bull and reef sharks, all of them bigger than her. "I'd only seen them in movies and in picture books," Ella told me. "When I saw my first shark up close, it was mind-blowing. They are more beautiful than any shark you've ever seen in a movie or book."

Her goal now is to visit—and help save—the Great Barrier Reef. Her favorite species is the whale shark. Her favorite fun fact about whale sharks is that their throats are really small, so they "can only swallow things as big as a grapefruit." While she was diving in Bimini, a Caribbean reef shark was determined to check out her camera. When Ella made eye contact with the shark, the shark swam away. "People look at them like they're these man-eating monsters, but they're really not."

Today she warns people about coral dying from climate change, overfishing and plastic pollution. She's trying to make sure we realize how much of that plastic comes from fishing. "Plastic pollution is going to affect generations after my generation. We need to fix this mess."

Instead of being scared of sharks, we should be terrified of losing them. Humans have walked on this planet for about 4 million years. Sharks have been swimming here for over 400 million years. They're ancient, beautiful, mysterious, curious and vital to the survival of the oceans, the atmosphere and us. We won't be here in 400 million years, or even 400, if sharks aren't here with us. We need to fight for a world we can share with sharks. That starts with replacing fear with respect and—just maybe—love.

A diver swims next to a whale shark in the Maldives.
CHRISTIAN JENSEN/FLICKR.COM/CC BY-SA 2.0

Julia Barnes goes to shark school.
KAREN BARNES

A DOZEN WAYS YOU CAN HELP SAVE SHARKS, THE SEAS AND US

WATCH WHAT YOU BUY

Check to make sure that the cat food, skin cream and suntan lotion you buy doesn't contain shark. If something contains squalene, make sure it isn't squalene from sharks. Many sunscreens poison coral reefs. If we can't eat these chemicals, neither can zooplankton or fish or sharks. Choose sunscreens that don't kill coral.

WATCH WHAT YOU EAT

Eating in an environmentally friendly way is complicated—even if you're vegan. If you eat fish, try to find out what you're eating and how it was caught. If tuna is your thing, stick to tuna caught by fishing poles, not longlines or trawlers. And make sure you don't eat too much because…mercury. Eating meat may also mean eating shark. Sort of. Forty percent of fish is caught to feed land animals to feed people.

Fish used to be considered the healthiest meat on the planet. Today most of the bigger fish that people enjoy eating come with a side of mercury and at least a pinch of microplastics. Different fish around the world are caught in different ways. Some fish are raised on farms. Some farms are well run. Others…not so much. So before you eat any fish—or feed it to your cats—try to find out more about it to make sure it's as safe as possible for you and the oceans. There are shark populations that some experts believe can be hunted in a sustainable way—but not many.

JOIN THE FIGHT TO MAKE SHARK FINNING ILLEGAL

The Fin Free movement keeps growing. Spread the word. If someone is selling shark-fin soup near you, support the people trying to stop them.

Sharks4Kids introduces sharks to kids and kids to sharks through scuba diving expeditions.
DUNCAN BRAKE/SHARKS4KIDS.COM

4

DONATE TO—OR RAISE MONEY FOR—GROUPS FIGHTING FOR SHARKS AND OCEAN HEALTH

I've shared the names of some great organizations in the resources section of this book, but look for people and groups doing work that inspires you.

5

BE AWARE OF WHAT YOU'RE THROWING "AWAY"

There is no "away." There are just oceans—which is where almost all our garbage ends up. Humans make a big mess. North Americans are traditionally the world's winners when it comes to creating garbage. The less trash we create, the better we're making the world for sharks and humans.

When I was a kid we used to worry about nuclear waste, because there's no safe way to get rid of it. Meanwhile, everything everywhere in my world was being replaced by plastic, and almost everyone thought that was awesome. Nobody seemed to realize that there's no way to dispose of plastic either.

One of the biggest sources of ocean plastic is "ghost gear." Fishing nets, long-lines and other fishing equipment that was cut loose or abandoned is one of the biggest sources of ocean pollution. We also dump poison into the water.

Chemicals we stopped using decades ago are still in the ocean. Fish are full of human medicine. And pesticides. Medicine needs to be properly disposed of. So do paints. Reduce. Reuse. Recycle. Repeat.

6

CONSIDER CLIMATE CHANGE

Scientists are freaking out over climate change and the impact it's having on our oceans. It's leading to ocean acidification—a condition caused when excess carbon dioxide turns water more acidic, which kills sea life like coral and zooplankton. Find out what you can do in your community to combat climate change.

SHARE THE RESOURCES

Humans like to claim we're the only beings on the planet who are altruistic and put the needs of others ahead of our own, but when we're looking at what we want to eat, we rarely worry about what other animals need to survive. Governments slaughter sharks who call the oceans home to keep beaches safe so that tourists can swim there on vacation. We look at all the life in the ocean as *our* food, *our* resources. Imagine if we shared the world. Imagine how much more amazing the world would be.

8

GET POLITICAL

Every community has environmental groups dealing with issues that affect our oceans. Find the issue that speaks to you and get involved. You can make a difference. Most politicians want people to love them. It doesn't matter how old you are—if you speak up about issues, you can make a difference. Write letters, make calls, volunteer for causes that matter to you. You can even start your own movement. There are young eco-heroes around the world. Join them.

Young environmentalists in action.
DUNCAN BRAKE/SHARKS4KIDS.COM

9

END ANTHROPODENIAL

Animals aren't things. Sharks may not be human, but don't pretend they're aliens. If an animal seems to be laughing, loving or in pain—assume they're laughing, loving or in pain.

10

KEEP LEARNING ABOUT SHARKS

One of my favourite internet tricks is setting Google news alerts so I get all the latest stories about issues that interest me. Set a Google news alert to get updates about your favorite sharks. I have alerts for orcas, whale sharks and Greenland sharks.

11

SHARE WHAT YOU LEARN

Don't be shy. People only protect what they love. Most people don't find sharks lovable—but they are *very* cool. Share your favorite shark facts. Tell your family. Tell your friends. Tell strangers. Write your own stories and books about sharks. Passion makes a difference. Passion inspires people. Some people will try to shut you down no matter what you say. It's the nature of the real world and the virtual one. They can tell their stories. Stay true to yours.

12

FIGHT GALEOPHOBIA!

Please share the fact that humans are more likely to be killed by dogs, cows and kangaroos than by a shark. We need to be less scared of seeing sharks in the ocean and more scared of *not* seeing sharks there. As long as people treat sharks like human-eating monsters, we won't do what needs to be done to save them. The oceans need sharks to survive and thrive, and so do we.

Sharks4Kids visits schools around the world to teach students about sharks, shark science and shark conservation.
JILLIAN MORRIS/SHARKS4KIDS.COM

GLOSSARY

ampullae of Lorenzini—tiny organs in a shark's head that detect electrical fields generated by other organisms

apex predators—the top predators in an area. This means that nothing in their neighborhood hunts them (except us).

baby shark—Baby shark, doo, doo, doo, doo, doo
Baby shark, doo, doo, doo, doo, doo

cartilage—tough yet flexible tissue (connected cells in the body of a living being) that weighs less and is more flexible than bone

Chondrichthyes—fish with skeletons made of cartilage, not bones

denticles—toothlike bumps that make up the skin of a shark

dorsal—the distinctive fin on a shark's back that helps them swim and turn

filter feeder—a subgroup of sharks who strain water to select the food they need

lateral lines—organs found on the sides of some sharks that help them sense movement and pressure changes in the water around them

nictitating membranes—eyelids that cover a shark's eyeballs when they're eating or fighting

nursery—a shallow and often protected area of water where mother sharks give birth and (usually) leave their babies to grow

pectoral—the fin on the side of a shark, just behind the gills

photophores—natural light-emitting organs found on some deep-sea fish

plankton—tiny animal and plant life in a body of water. Plankton is the fave food of filter-feeding sharks. There are two types of plankton: Phytoplankton are tiny plants known as algae. Zooplankton are tiny fish, krill and many other species without backbones.

spiracles—small holes behind the eyes of some sharks that help them breathe when they are resting on the seabed or buried in sand and silt

squalene—oil found in the liver of a shark and also in some plants

sustainable—capable of being continued by not taking more from nature than can be replenished by nature and/or with human help

RESOURCES

PRINT

Eilperin, Juliet. *Demon Fish: Travels Through the Hidden World of Sharks*. Penguin Random House, 2011.

Keating, Jess. *Shark Lady: The True Story of How Eugenie Clark Became the Ocean's Most Fearless Scientist*. Sourcebooks, 2017.

McKeever, William. *Emperors of the Deep: Sharks—The Ocean's Most Mysterious, Most Misunderstood, and Most Important Guardians*. HarperCollins, 2019.

Morris, Jillian. *Norman the Nurse Shark*. Sharks4Kids Inc, 2017.

Ramsey, Ocean. *What You Should Know about Sharks: Shark Language, Social Behavior, Human Interactions, and Life-Saving Information*. Independently published, 2019.

Skerry, Brian. *The Ultimate Book of Sharks*. National Geographic Kids, 2018.

ONLINE

Bimini Sharklab: biminisharklab.com

Fins Attached: finsattached.org

FishBase (A Global Information System on Fishes): fishbase.de/home.htm

Global Finprint (the world's largest reef shark and ray survey): globalfinprint.org

Humane Society International Canada: hsi.org/issues/shark-finning

International Shark Attack File: floridamuseum.ufl.edu/shark-attacks

MarineSafe: marinesafe.org

Mission Blue: mission-blue.org/about

National Geographic: nationalgeographic.com

Project Hiu: projecthiu.com

Rob Stewart Sharkwater Foundation:
    robstewartsharkwaterfoundation.org
Save the Reef: savethereef.org
The SeaChange Agency: theseachangeagency.org
Sea Shepherd: seashepherdglobal.org
Sea Walls: Artists for Oceans: seawalls.org/murals
Shark Conservation Australia: sharkconservation.org.au
Sharks in Canada: sharksincanada.ca
Sharks4Kids: sharks4kids.com
Smithsonian: ocean.si.edu
The Sharkwater VR Experience:
    sharkwater.com/sharkwater-extinction/videos/vr-experience/
World Wildlife: worldwildlife.org

DOCUMENTARIES

Delafosse, Jérôme, dir. *Saving Sharks: Raising Awareness*. 2015;
    United States, MagellanTV.
Barnes, Julia, dir. *Sea of Life*. 2017; Canada, Oceanic Productions.
    seaoflifemovie.com
Kaufmann, Gisella, dir. *Shark Girl*. 2014; Australia,
    Kaufmann Productions. Smithsonian channel TV movie.
    kaufmannproductions.com
Stewart, Rob, dir. *Revolution*. 2012; Canada, Revolutionary Films Inc.
    therevolutionmovie.com
Stewart, Rob, dir. *Sharkwater*. 2006; Canada, Sharkwater
    Productions. sharkwater.com
Stewart, Rob, dir. *Sharkwater Extinction*. 2018; Canada,
    Sharkwater Productions. sharkwater.com

* *United Conservationists/Rob Stewart Sharkwater Foundation grants free
license usage of Rob's films for educational uses.*

PODCASTS

Let's Talk Shark by Erich Ritter: letstalkshark.com
Shark Stories by Madison Stewart
Skaana: skaana.org

Links to external resources are for personal and/or educational use only and are provided in good faith without any express or implied warranty. There is no guarantee given as to the accuracy or currency of any individual item. The author and publisher provide links as a service to readers. This does not imply any endorsement by the author or publisher of any of the content accessed through these links.

ACKNOWLEDGMENTS

When I started writing about Moby Doll—the first orca displayed in captivity—I met a lot of incredible scientists, researchers, activists and animal lovers. After I finished the book, these people kept telling me stories the world needed to know. My wife, Rayne Benu, said we should do a podcast to help them share these stories with the world and that she was game to produce it. In 2017 *Skaana* was born.

When Rob Stewart's final movie, *Sharkwater Extinction*, was set to debut in 2018, I wanted to do all I could to help promote it and honor his vision and his life. My friend Katherine Dodds was listening to *Skaana* and heard me mention that I was airing an old interview I'd done with Rob. She was promoting *Sharkwater Extinction* and asked if I'd be the person who connected with environmental organizations to make sure the movie did what it was meant to and helped save sharks. After I wrote three books for young readers about whales for Orca Book Publishers, my editors asked if I'd like to write about another animal. Yes, I said—sharks. It has to be sharks.

And from the moment I started working on this, the *Sharkwater* team was there for me, providing not only information and connections to experts, but also some of the most astonishing photos in this book. So a very special thanks to Rob's parents, Brian and Sandy Stewart, and to Carrie Wolfe, who fielded my questions for the Rob Stewart Sharkwater Foundation.

Because I teach the occasional class at the University of Victoria, I often work with UVic students on my projects. This book wouldn't exist without the *Skaana* podcast team—a crew Rayne and I connected with through UVic—including Katie Brown, Liz Flick-Belus and Izabella Almasi. Through my UVic work, I was lucky enough to meet with researcher Thayne Harden and researcher and writer Brian Murphy. Brian didn't just assist with research and fact-checking, but was my designated shark-image hunter.

Many *Skaana* interviews are part of this book. I've included quotes, information and ideas from conversations that changed the way I see the world. This includes talks with David Suzuki, Lori Marino, Carl Safina, Daniel Pauly, Erich Hoyt, Peter Wohlleben, Kriss Kevorkian and Fin Donnelly. Many of these experts answered questions for me for this book. *Skaana* guest Frans de Waal rocked my world with his work around anthropodenial. If there's one thing I hope you remember from this book—besides that sharks aren't trying to kill you and the world needs them—it's the idea that if we want to save the species we share this planet with, we need to fight anthropodenial.

This book would not exist without the help of Sea Shepherd captain Paul Watson, author Marc Bekoff, Michael Millstein and Heidi Dewar from NOAA, author and photographer Alessandro De Maddalena, shark-lover and eco-activist Ella Grace, and filmmakers and world-changers Julia Barnes and Madison Stewart. I'd also like to add thanks to Gavin Naylor and Tyler Bowling from the Florida Program for Shark Research, which manages the International Shark Attack File.

Special whale-shark-sized thanks to Gavin Hanke, curator of vertebrate zoology at the Royal BC Museum, for all his support, patience and especially his help translating some of the science for me.

Thank you to Orca publishers Andrew Woolridge and Ruth Linka for inviting me to play in the Orca pool and continuing to ask, "What else would you like to write?" Thanks to editor Kirstie Hudson and editorial assistant Georgia Bradburne for all their help in bringing this book to life, and designer Jenn Playford for working her magic to share the beauty of sharks and their environment. And thanks to everyone at Orca for all the love and care you put into this book and all the others you send into the world.

And, above all, thanks to the always awesome Rayne Benu, for her love and support, and for convincing me that some stories have to be shared.

Do these sharks really look scary to you?
ANDREW GRAY, NOAA/FLICKR.COM/PUBLIC DOMAIN

INDEX

*Page numbers in **bold** indicate an image caption.*

A snorkeler visits a tiger shark in West End, Bahamas.
STEPHEN FRINK/GETTY IMAGES